French Letters

by

George East

Illustrations by Robin Evans

Plan of La Puce by Con Barnes

French Letters

Published by
La Puce Publications
87 Laburnum Grove
North End
Portsmouth PO2 0HG

Telephone: (023) 92 678148
Facsimile: (023) 92 665070

First Impression 1999
Second printing 2000
Third printing 2001
This edition 2002

ISBN 0 9523635 2 6

Designed and typeset by Nigel at Christianson Hoper Norman
Reprographics by SP Digital
Printed in Great Britain by Borcombe Printers PLC, Hampshire

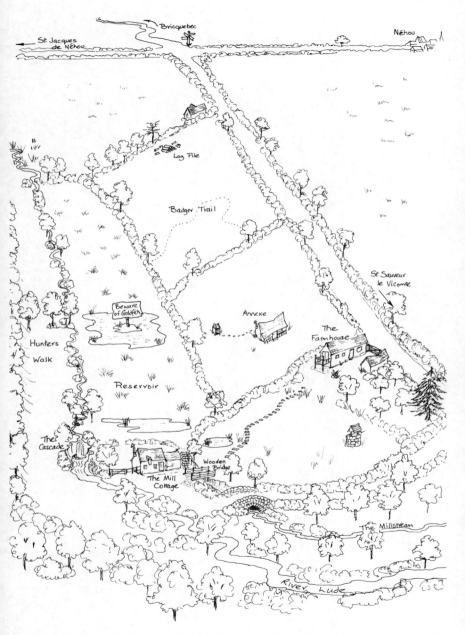

La Puce and the Mill Of The Flea

For my mother

Author's Note

This mish-mash of a book is in response to public demand; most pleasingly from regular readers, but most urgently from my bank manager and other long-term creditors. All the following stories are true except for the ones that aren't, and were either experienced first-hand or passed on by others with a similar appreciation of the bizarre. Where necessary, names and locations have been changed to avoid possible embarrassment and almost certain legal action. As to the traditional dedications and thanks for all the people who made this great work possible, they are too many to mention and will anyway know who they are.

Across the years of our adventuring in France I have observed that there are certain similarities between the sort of people who, like us, like messing about in someone else's country. We have met bricklayers, barristers and even the odd retired burglar on our travels, and regardless of their differing backgrounds and circumstances, all seem to share certain character traits and attitudes. They are the sort of people who, in past centuries, would have been found half way up an Amazonian creek without a paddle, or more probably without even a boat. Most of all, they seem to share the same lust for learning from their mistakes, and in the process learning about themselves as well as other cultures and people. They also like to laugh, perhaps because it is the best or sometimes only option.

French Letters is therefore dedicated to all those who, like us, have learned that while it may sometimes be better to travel in hope than to actually arrive, the journey can often be worthwhile. Always providing you are able to laugh about the horrendous cock-ups you make *en route*.

The story so far

Following a series of disastrous financial excursions, failed bed tester, radio DJ and pickled onion manufacturer George East fled with his wife Donella to the Mill of the Flea in Normandy's Cherbourg peninsula. After spectacular failures with a series of schemes, the couple found a measure of fame if not fortune with *Home & Dry in France* and *René & Me*. Moving on to their land and in to the couple's lives shortly after their arrival in Cotentin, René Ribet is still the Easts' self-appointed estate manager and guide to the ways of the French countryside and people. To the locals and those who have had financial dealings with him, Mr Ribet is known as The Fox of Cotentin.

The Cotentin occupies most of the Cherbourg peninsula, and is the top bit of the *département* of Manche, which is part of Lower Normandy. A land of mists and myths, the Cotentin is in the queue claiming to be the true birthplace of King Arthur, and it is indisputably a place of magic to those who discover its real charm.

The village of Néhou lies in the heart of the Cotentin, has one shop, a garage, a church and a population of around three hundred. It is as like and unlike any other small rural community as it is possible to imagine.

Linguistic Note

Curiously, French slang for a condom is *une capote anglaise*, or 'English greatcoat'. Following French logic, the item is of the feminine gender; why our oldest enemies should choose to be so flattering as to suggest we would need a prophylactic the size of an overcoat is yet another gallic mystery. Incidentally, if you should ever have need of wood preservative while in France, don't make the same mistake as I did on an early visit to the local DIY centre. *Préservatif* is proper French for French letter, if you see what I mean.

Friends and books should be few but good.

Norman proverb

Singing for England

It is the week before Christmas, and raining steadily as we drive
to the carol service. Rain is more than common in the Cotentin,
but this is serious stuff. Even the deep roadside ditches are
struggling to cope, and the local soothsayers are making grim
forecasts of the worst floods in living memory. They make the
same prediction every year, but this time I think they may be right.

We turn off the main road to cross the old stone bridge spanning
the River Douve, and I see that things are indeed getting out of
hand. A flash of lightning illuminates the turbulent scene below
and the probing fingers of muddy water reaching out to a riverside
farm. It won't be long before the Douve has the single-storey
building in its clutch, explaining the local expression about farmers
wearing their rubber boots to bed in the rainy season.

Victor the Volvo struggles manfully up the winding road from the
lowlands of the Douve to the hilltop village of Fierville-les-Mines,
and the church where the carol service is to be held appears,
dramatically silhouetted against the brooding night sky by another
flash of lightning. As if by a miracle, it stops raining as we reach
the square, and we are touched to see that a convenient sycamore
tree has been draped with fairy lights to mark the occasion. There
are already many cars parked in the square, and I note from the
registration plates that the English and French are keeping their
distance at either end of the square. I am sure things will be much
more inter-denominational in the church.

Leaving Victor parked pointedly mid-way between the two camps, we squelch along the path leading to the church, and I am glad we are wearing our warmest clothing. Donella has made a concession to the occasion by wearing her best wellington boots and a clean bobble-cap, and I have been persuaded to leave my Father Christmas hat at home. Threading our way between the gravestones and towards the welcoming light of the church portals, we say hello to several English friends, and see other obvious expatriots who we have not as yet met.

Inside, we realise that it is going to be a full house, and a divided one. Although the French and English ushers at the door invite us to sit where we will as they hand out the dual language songsheets, we find ourselves on the side of the aisle which has obviously been colonised by the British contingent. Settling down while the last stragglers are ushered in, I look around and reflect on the typically French approach to the maintenance and décor of this sturdy Norman church. Solidly constructed of stone from the quarry for which the village is named, the interior of the church is as ornate as the exterior is plain. It is also very religious. Ancient frescoes forming a frieze around the walls depict the stations of the cross, and a giant brass crucifix dominates the altar. Above us, the candlelight reflects dully from the sleek bodies of a pair of brazen eagles perched high on either side of the pulpit. In stark contrast, a series of ugly gas-fed panels bodged on to the fluted stone columns provide the only source of heating, and I cannot help noticing that only half the heaters on the English side of the church have been lit.

After the usual coughing and shuffling, two figures appear at the altar. One in full ecclesiastical fig and obviously on home ground, while the other is wearing a sensible and very British waxed jacket and an immaculate tweed suit. The effect is somewhat marred by a pair of Eskimo-type padded bootees; like all English settlers in Cotentin, he has obviously learned the value of compromising between style and comfort during a long and cold winter.

11

After waiting for silence, which takes much longer on the French side of the aisle, our hosts welcome us to the church and annual carol service, with the waxed jacket speaking in French, and his remarks being translated by the curé immediately afterwards. It is a nice touch, but I can't help being put in mind of the Eurovision song contest.

Following the opening remarks, it is time for the first carol, and the curé of Fierville explains that we are going to alternate the service, with an English carol followed by a French one. For our convenience, we will find the translation printed alongside in each case, and he hopes we will all sing along in the appropriate language. We all nod earnestly and there is much throat-clearing as the massed bands of the local fire brigade and school strike up the familiar - at least to us - opening chords of *Once in Royal David's City*. As I concentrate on finding approximately the note and my wife shuffles away from my side in deep embarrassment, it becomes clear that we are not getting much support from those on the French side of the church. Most seem to be moving their lips and at least trying to mime the English words, but few are actually attempting to sing them. There has also been an awkward moment at the start, as the entire English congregation rose to their feet as the music began, while the French community stayed firmly rooted to their seats. This resulted in some confusion as a number of our hosts quickly stood up, while about half of us sat down. Eventually an awkward compromise was reached, with the English half-crouching and the French sitting up straight.

Now it is time to air the first French carol, which according to my song sheet is called *Il Est Ne Le Divin Enfant*. On comforting home territory, the band strikes up with gusto, and their enthusiasm is matched by the French congregation. Regrettably, the response from the English side is not so fulsome, and we receive some sour looks from across the aisle.

This seems to have set the pattern for the evening, with each side of the great divide ripping into their own familiar carols, then mumbling half-heartedly and sometimes resentfully through the foreign variety.

While not wishing to takes sides, I have to say that our carols seem somehow much more Christmassy, with *The Holly and The Ivy* and *God Rest Ye Merry Gentlemen* streets ahead of *Dans Cette Etable* and *Venez, Divin Messie* in terms of overall melody and jollity. Like the church itself, the French songs seem to concentrate overly on the solemn and even gloomy aspects of Christianity and the founder's birthday.

We have now reached the grand finale, and our representative announces somewhat nervously and in English that the last carol is going to be a truly joint effort. If we turn to the last page in our song sheets, we will see that the song is to be *O Come All Ye Faithful*. To exemplify the Christmas spirit of reconciliation and togetherness, this time we will all join together in performing this traditional carol entirely in Latin.

During his translation for the benefit of the French congregation, I note that the curé adds a little to our man's address by exorting his flock to give of their best and show their guests how well they can sing. He stops short of adding 'for the honour of France', but does slip in reference to the fact that Latin was and, unlike some other newer branches of Christianity, still is the official language of the True Church.

The good curé of Fierville has apparently forgotten that at least half the English congregation are quite familiar with the French language, and there are some mutterings as the throat-clearing and coughing reaches a crescendo and the band strikes up.

All goes reasonably well for the first verse, then someone on our side of the aisle appears to forget the rules, and breaks into English during the chorus. After the next verse, the whole row joins the rebel, and there is an instant response from across the aisle. From this point on, every time we reach the chorus we sing in our own tongue, with each side triumphantly and joyfully taking on the old enemy. Meanwhile, the choir and the curé are sticking religiously to the Latin, and our man in the tweed suit is obviously wavering. The overall result of the friendly competition is that everyone is singing at the tops of their voices, and the noise level seems enough to wake those villagers resting in eternal peace just beyond the vibrating oak doors.

During the final thundering chorus, I see the curé look up warily at the vaulted ceiling, and a faint shower of dust settles on his caped shoulders as we reach our ear-shattering conclusion.

*   *   *   *   *

The congregation is moving through the darkened streets of Fierville-les-Mines towards the village hall, and the silence is almost deafening. It is not so much that nobody wishes to speak, but that most are too hoarse to hold a prolonged conversation. Like battle-weary troops, we trudge wordlessly beneath the Christmas stars to where our differences will be forgotten as we share a festive drink.

Unfortunately, we arrive at the *salle* to find that the laying out of the food and drink has been as unintentionally divisive as the seating arrangements at the church. At one end of the hall, our French hosts have put on a spectacular spread, while the trestle table at the other end bears the much simpler contribution from the English Goodwill committee. Clearly, our representatives have contented themselves with piles of traditional mince pies, a small Christmas cake and some punchbowls containing mulled and spiced ale. At the other end, the French table looks like the winning entry in the Paris *salon culinaire*, with every variety of sweetmeat, cake and exquisite delicacy artfully displayed.

On entering the hall, each of us goes instinctively to the French or English end of the hall, and we stand looking at each other like two opposing armies waiting for the off. Our man and the curé of Fierville are now stranded in the middle of no-mans-land, and I do not help matters by trying to break the ice and suggesting a game of British Bulldog before we start on the refreshments.

*   *   *   *   *

Later, and the situation has been resolved. The good food and drink has worked its magic, and past differences in the church were forgiven if not forgotten as the two sides came together to celebrate rather than dwell on our disparate cultures and attitudes. So far, none of our hosts has made even a single reference to the outcome of the World Cup, and we have begun to party in earnest as the musical entertainment begins. Fierville has its own disc jockey and he has an even wider collection of 70's disco hits than our own Néhou Kid. As my wife teaches the curé to dance The Shag, I top up my glass of mulled ale and take a breather from the fray.

Outside, a million stars jostle for attention in a crowded yet cloudless sky, and it is hard to believe that more rain is forecast for tomorrow. I look at the distant planets and find it hard to believe there is no life on a single one of them. Perhaps somewhere out there in the boundless reaches of the galaxy, a strange creature is even now looking at our tiny planet and wondering if life exists here, and what form it could take. I shall never know, but am sure of one thing. However vivid any alien's imagination might be, I think he would be very hard put to come up with as much as an inkling of what life is like for us here in our small corner of the Universe.

Eyes Down for a Full House

I t could only happen to us.

When we arrived in the village hall, all seemed ready for the yearly Christmas knees-up. The temporary bar was fully stocked with a lethal collection of home-brew Calvados disguised as lemonade bottles, and our disc jockey The Néhou Kid was earnestly polishing his one-record collection of *Greatest Disco Hits In The World Ever! (1969-70)*. Already, the hall was jammed with enough tables and bench seats to accommodate the entire community, and the sturdy figures of freshly-shaven and scrubbed villagers were busy laying claim to the best seats in the house. Their husbands were also dressed up to the nines.

But something was missing.

The tables were unlaid, and the kitchen doors firmly shut. And where was the usual fever of activity and delightfully conflicting aromas signposting the journey of culinary exploration we would be taking? Worse still, why was our legendary superchef JayPay blowing tentatively into the local DJ's microphone rather than on to a ladle of gently steaming *potage paysan*?

A hurried conversation with our new mayor revealed that we were here under false pretences. When Madame Ghislaine asked us if we would be attending the village *bal*, we should have suspected something when she didn't lock us in till we bought our tickets. Proprietor of the local bar and grocery shop and president and sole member of the Néhou Retailers Association, Ghislaine is a ferocious fund-raiser for the village school. She is also convinced that we, like all Britons mad enough to buy a ruin in France, are eccentric millionaires. Her sales pitch invariably comes at the close of our first Sunday morning session in the Bar Ghislaine after one of our own fund-raising trips to England. With our euphoria level at its height and our resistance conversely low, Ghislaine knows that I will buy at least a dozen tickets for every raffle, draw and event in progress, and there are often as many as four a week. So far we have not been lucky in any of the sweepstakes, but came close to winning the hind quarters of a prematurely retired (due to the small matter of a missing leg) trotting pony last summer.

As the mayor now explains, I must have misheard Madame Ghislaine due to my unfamiliarity with basic French as it is spoken in this area. We are not gathered in the village hall for a ball, but to *play* the balls.

In other words, it is bingo night at Néhou.

Rather than looking contentedly at a full plate, it will be eyes down for a full *maison*. As René rather wittily observes when I tell him of the error, it seems as if we have made a real balls-up of the evening.

*   *   *   *   *

The session is now in full swing, and the atmosphere is far from *amiable*.

It appears that the scale and level of prizes has attracted travelling pot-hunters, some from as far away as Valognes, which is all of ten miles distant. Apart from their unfamilar faces and city-slicker cardigans, the visitors are instantly identifiable by their professional approach to the game and their state-of-the art equipment. Our local players have handfuls of buttons and ten centime coins to blank out the numbers on their cards, while René has persuaded me to buy a whole pack of beer so that we can use the bottle tops. The strangers are armed with little metal discs which are picked up with a stylish magnetised wand after each game. Next to us on the table nearest to the calling station is a serious-looking family of eight, each of whom has claimed the maximum of four cards per player. One of the children is still in his mother's arms, and there has been quite a to-do about whether he is qualified to take part. The mayor was called in to adjudicate before the games could commence, and he has reluctantly agreed that the advertising posters did not stipulate an age limit. He has, however, refused to allow the family's fox-terrier to play.

With the dispute settled, we start the first game, and I immediately realise we are going to have a problem in keeping up with the action. As the most respected person in the community, JayPay is our caller, and while he is the undisputed master of all things culinary, his microphone technique leaves much to be desired. Being a perfectionist in all things, he has taken an intensive training course from our local DJ, and is therefore almost unintelligible. Apart from adopting the nasal sing-song style favoured by disc-jockeys everywhere, he is speaking at his usual machine-gun rate, and is using patois for the jokey remarks accompanying each call. Deciphering the numbers he is pulling from the drum is proving near-impossible even for the locals, as JayPay is now affecting a pseudo-American accent which does not fit well with his broad Cotentinese. Neither my wife nor I would know the local equivalent of Two Little Ducks or Doctor's Orders even if we could understand what our caller is saying, and René is not proving much of a help.

Apart from the twelve cards he bought with my 500 franc note, he has now ordered two more packs of beer so that we can use the caps as markers. My suggestion that we can re-use the same bottle tops for each game is turned down out of hand as tradition dictates this to be unlucky. The Fox also insists on following his own traditions by emptying each bottle before using the cap.

As the evening progresses, the situation becomes even more stressful. The bounty-hunting family alongside us has already won a hand-axe, a pair of designer wellington boots and a live chicken, and feelings are running high. For the sake of accord, I hope that the foreigners do not win the evening's star prize, which is an almost-new chain saw, complete with a bottle of lubricating oil and first-aid kit. Although all profits from the session will go to the school, the organisers and villagers like to see the prizes stay in the community. Our table is also the focus of additional hostility because René is proving increasingly difficult. Having started on a third pack of bottle tops, he is now querying every call that JayPay makes, and has even offered to take over the microphone. It can't be long before Ribet The Fox takes to the table-top for his notorious Whirling Dervish routine.

I ease the tension by taking René's cards over and sending him to buy another pack of beer, and our fortunes change almost immediately. The next prize is a framed painting of the church at Néhou, and we appear to be well in the running as more and more of our numbers come up. We still cannot understand JayPay's transatlantic patois, but the ever-practical Madame Ghislaine has come up with a solution. She has equipped herself with a marker pen and a supply of hastily-assembled squares of cardboard torn from the prize packaging. Standing on a chair behind our caller, she is looking over his shoulder and noting the numbers as they come out of the drum, scribbling them on a card, then holding it up for all to see.

Unaware of the situation and hearing no further complaints from the audience, JayPay is reaching new heights of unintelligibility and excess with his delivery. It also looks as if we are close to a result, and the winner may well come from our table. Sneaking a look at the pot-hunting family's cards, I see that the baby has only two uncovered spaces, while we are just my lucky number seven away from snatching the prize.

Having returned with our latest supply of bottle tops and appraised himself of the situation, René has gone around the hall with the news, and excitement is reaching fever-pitch. Although the villagers, being Norman, would naturally prefer to win any prizes for themselves, a picture of the place they visit religiously every Sunday is not a great catch. However, they would obviously much prefer to see it won by honorary locals like us rather than total strangers.

As we wait in breathless silence, JayPay reaches a huge hand into the drum, rummages around to show fair play, then takes out a ping-pong ball. As he goes into overdrive with the build-up to his announcement, Madame Ghislaine writes swiftly on a card and holds the number up. It is, I see, a seven.

Caught up in the excitement, I leap to my feet, and after some rapid mental translation, shout *'C'est moi - maison pleine!'*

At first there is no reaction, then seats scrape around the hall as almost the entire audience gets to its feet. For a moment, I think the villagers are going to give me a standing ovation for defeating the pot-hunting family, but soon realise they are merely taking the opportunity to visit the bar or toilets while my numbers are checked.

As an official takes our card for inspection and verification, René arrives from the bar to say that my triumphant full house shout has been misinterpreted. The expression is unknown in French bingo circles, he explains, and predicts with grim relish that I will shortly be besieged as a result of my outburst. Having seen us spend a considerable fortune on changing a perfectly sound cattle shed at La Puce into a cottage and registered with disbelief the sums other settlers from the UK have spent on local houses, everyone in Néhou is convinced that all English people are completely mad when it comes to property speculation. According to our friend, a number of the audience will have taken my strangled shout as a cry for help and a plea for a further fix to satisfy my cravings to buy ruins at vastly inflated prices and throw lots of money at them. As a result, he says, at least six local farmers will shortly be approaching me with invitations to buy their unwanted outbuildings.

It later transpires that René has only been making a rather laboured joke, but it also appears that we have not, in fact, won the painting of the church. There follows an embarrassing moment as Madame Ghislaine goes through my card and discovers that I have not got a full house, or anything like it.

Half of the numbers covered by René have as yet to be called, as has my lucky winning number. In the excitement, I had forgotten that the French way of distinguishing a number one is to put a tail on the top of the vertical stroke, and had mistaken Madame Ghislaine's final card for a seven. I make a public apology, but worse is to follow as the interrupted game continues and the baby swiftly fills his two remaining spaces.

*   *   *   *   *

The *bal* is over, and we are walking back to La Puce. Normally, we would have been offered a lift in a passing car or tractor, but we are in disgrace. Because of the misunderstanding over my claim to the picture of the church at Néhou, the villagers seem to hold me responsible for the pot-hunting foreigners winning yet another prize. As if that were not bad enough, there was nearly an outbreak of violence when the head of family asked if he could swap the picture for another prize, even one of less value. He said he thought the church particularly unattractive and the execution of the painting even worse. This double insult to the standards of local architecture and the skills of our resident artist was one thing; the revelation that the family are new residents of our rival village of St Jacques de Néhou was too much to bear.

After the mayor had calmed things down and convened the inevitable committee meeting, the foreigners were allowed to keep their prizes on the condition that they accepted the painting of the church, apologised to the artist and left before the game for the star prize. It did not help matters that the winner of the coveted chain saw was our friend René Ribet, who had craftily taken over the cards abandoned by the pot-hunters.

We hurry across the main road and climb the broken gate to our top fields. In contrast to the angry scenes at the village hall, all is peaceful as we pause to look at the reflection of the buttery Norman moon on the calm surface of the big pond. Ronnie and Reggie Crayfish and their gang are safely banged up for the winter, and most of our other residents are sleeping or have gone off to warmer climes till Spring returns. In the distance, an owl hoots as if in derision of our performance at our first Cotentinese bingo session, and I hear the unmistakeable buzz of René's moped as he weaves down the old cart track to our mill cottage.

Doubtless, our visitor will be in search of a nightcap, and the opportunity to sell me his newly acquired chain saw. As he will surely point out before closing the deal, we will need a newer model to replace the one which went missing from the tool shed at La Puce during our last visit to England.

On The Waterfront

I have been taking an early stroll around the estate, and find that an unexpected frost has turned La Puce into a Christmas card.

During the night, a giant hand has been sprinkling icing sugar across the fields, and the air is so cold and sharp that I might have been sucking a whole tube of extra-strong mints. Filling my lungs, I fleetingly consider the benefits of giving up the roll-ups, then regain my senses and sit by the jetty for a contemplative smoke.

One of the great pleasures of taking on such a sizeable amount of neglected land is that I have enough work not to do at La Puce to last the rest of my life. Although our dear friend the late mayor of Néhou kept the upper fields and hedges in immaculate condition, he left the unworkable land, trees and waterways in our hands, and we have left their care to mother nature. She knows much more than us about keeping things in order and her labour comes free, so we are content to leave her to her work. The odd tree falls across the river, and we have an interesting new swamp at the end of the water meadow as a result of a huge beech branch causing the *Lude* to overflow. As Donella says, it would have cost a small fortune to build it ourselves, and will provide a new housing estate for the overspill from the big pond, where over-population and turf wars are becoming a major problem. There have been outbreaks of bloody violence all summer, and we are actually beginning to feel sorry for the normally ferocious crayfish gang.

When I first suggested introducing goldfish to the big pond to see if they would sink or swim, my wife was horrified. Though Trevor the lone trout has proved man enough to stand his ground, she could not bear the thought of providing bite-sized snacks for the Cray twins and their mob. Consequently, I made a secret trip to the small pond one night while Donella was on a badger-spotting mission, and transferred Psycho the goldfish and a dozen or so of his harem to their new quarters. We originally inherited Psycho from friends who said he had killed off two very expensive Siamese fighting fish when they had put him in their tropical tank while cleaning out his bowl, and he has certainly lived up to his name.

Three years on, and there are now at least two hundred oddly coloured members of the *carassius auratus* family living in the big pond, and all seem to have inherited the psychotic genes of their ancestor. Being so inbred, I suppose it is only natural that they should exhibit unnatural characteristics. Rather than swim aimlessly about on their own as other goldfish do, they invariably cruise menacingly just below the surface in a spear-shaped flotilla. The whole tribe also seems to be utterly fearless and permanently ravenous, and I have long since abandoned my yearly dip in the big pond. Once undisputed lords of their manor, the individual members of the crayfish gang now seem loath to challenge the Psycho tribe's authority, and have even taken to going around in pairs.

The goldfish also seem to completely disregard the basic rules and regulations of sleeping the winter away. Though, like the crays, they are not normally in evidence from late autumn onwards, their genetic mutation seems to have included a gift for greatly enhanced hearing. I noticed this last summer during a re-stocking visit to the caravan, which has long been given over to a feeding station rivalling any supermarket for range and quality of products. Unlike the usual system, our customers pay nothing for their weekly groceries. While Donella and I were having words about my proposals for cutting back by withdrawing some of the luxury items or at least supplying cheaper brands of cheeses and smoked sausage, we noticed a stir by the island. A scout having spotted us and spread the word, the Psycho flotilla was soon under way, leaving a wake like a torpedo as it made for the bank. Within minutes, my wife had emptied a jar of floating fish sticks and disposed of two rounds of top-grade camembert cheese, and the water was boiling like a cauldron as the feeding frenzy reached its peak. I actually saw a tiny black and white goldfish with an ugly scar down its cheek headbutt a crayfish twice its size for just daring to join in the orgy, and it would have been a brave man who would have ventured to put his fingers into the maelstrom.

The ritual having been established, Donella now visits the big pond every day and calls the Psycho tribe to dine, and I take great care not to cough when having a quiet smoke by the jetty lest I wake them.

As I stand to leave the tranquil winter setting, I hear a flutter from behind the giant gunnera plants lining the far bank of the pond, and see that our overfed heron is regarding me reproachfully. Hector arrived at La Puce and the big pond two summers ago, and immediately became yet another non-paying guest. When I first disturbed him, he observed the niceties of the normal heron-human relationship and flapped off resentfully to other stops on his daily route. Nowadays, he seems to spend all his time by the big pond, and to regard my appearance as an intrusion on his privacy. Within weeks of his arrival, I noticed that he was putting on weight, and seemed to have increasing difficulty in getting airborne without a long and abnormally ponderous run-up. At first, I thought he was wreaking havoc amongst the goldfish, and admired him for his bravery in taking them on. Later, I noticed that he seemed strangely reluctant to wade far enough into the water to get into striking distance, and his obvious corpulence remained a mystery until I discovered a pile of rusting sardine cans hidden beneath a giant leaf in the gunnera rainforest.

As I turn to make my way back to the mill cottage, I nod sympathetically to Hector as he nervously eyes the shallows of the big pond. It's just as well that he no longer has to rely on traditional fishing activities for his daily intake. This morning I don't have the keys to the caravan with me, but will remember to tell my wife that a hungry resident is waiting for his breakfast.

*   *   *   *   *

It is Christmas Day, and I have been to see my darling Lucky.

He left us almost exactly a year ago, and it is the first time I have been able to bring myself to go and sit where my old friend sleeps beneath a tree on Hunter's Walk. It was his favourite cool spot to rest after a long summer's day chasing imaginary rabbits in the water meadow, and is a peaceful place for him to lie forever.

Although my wife loved him as much as I, she always said that he was my dog, and would thoughtfully make an excuse when I suggested we all take a walk together. Usually, Lucky and I would go to the woods behind St Sauveur, where the council had spent a Euro-grant to build a jogging circuit so that local people could keep fit. Predictably, the idea of dressing up in a track suit and swinging from parallel bars to improve their muscle-tone held little appeal for the citizens of St Sauveur, so we always had the place completely to ourselves. In the last months we shared our daily walk, I noticed that Lucky was slowing down, and one day, he just sat in the car and looked at me when I called him. When he stopped eating, we took him to the vet already knowing what she would say, and leaving him there was the hardest decision we have ever had to make. As we held him in our arms, he looked at me and I knew that he understood. While I waited in the car afterwards, Donella cut some of the lovely golden feathered hair from his legs, and she says she will be happy to sell La Puce and everything we own to pay to have my dog cloned when science makes it possible.

I thought the pain would go away with time, but it has not. Sometimes, I wake in the night and think I feel his comforting weight at the foot of the bed, but he is not there. Of all the dogs we have loved across the years, he was somehow special, and I shall never forget him.

Good boy, Lucky. Sleep tight.

Pension Plan

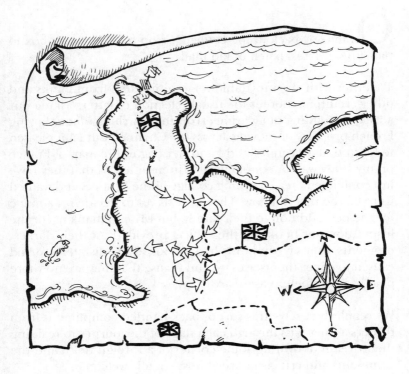

O n my way back to the cottage, I stop off at the post box to pick up our latest batch of fan mail.

Together with the inevitable terse reminders from banks and other creditors, there is the usual selection of letters asking our advice or pointing out glaring errors in my writings about buying French property or moving across the Channel. But I am pleased to learn that we can now add another flag to the map of France on my study wall. A couple have written to tell us that they have just completed on a charming cottage in the Vendée, and wanted us to be the first to know. They have as yet to decide on a name for the new addition to their family, but write to thank us for the inspiration our books on the subject provided. At their darkest moments, they say, they only had to look at the disasters we had caused to cheer themselves up and realise that they are nowhere near as incompetent as we are.

We regularly receive this sort of back-handed compliment from readers as they pass through each stage of the journey to realising their dream of owning some corner of a foreign field, and the comments and criticisms are almost equally welcome.

We like nothing better at this time of year than to sit by the fire in the mill cottage and read how our correspondents are getting on. For us, it is a wonderful opportunity to re-live our own emotions and adventures in the early days, and there may be a practical bonus for our old age.

There are 91 *départements* in France. Most, with some notably French and therefore bewildering exceptions, are sensibly numbered in approximate alphabetical order. The department of Ain, for example, is number 1, while we in Manche are awarded a 50, and Yonne is number 89. The department of Belfort, for what I am sure are its own very good reasons, lays claim to number 90.

The map on my study wall bears a flag for every department where at least one of our correspondents has bought a home and settled, and been rash enough to offer us unstinted hospitality if we ever happen to be in their area. Little do they know that I have devised a foolproof scheme for taking advantage of their kind offers while spending the autumn of our years living and travelling in France for next-to-nothing. If my wife agrees, we will make out a carefully planned route to encompass all participating departments, then turn up on the doorstep of the first with a bottle of wine and an overnight bag. Having worn out our welcome, it will be time to move on to the next host on the list. So far, there are 57 flags sprouting from the map, which should mean we will not have to strain any individual host's tolerance for even a week.

*　　*　　*　　*　　*

Apart from the new addition to my pension plan club, I also see that we have a letter from Moondance and Zak, the pen-names of two readers who have recently moved to France. In my experience, they seem just the sort of couple to adapt, survive and even prosper in the new life they have chosen.

Like us, they would probably be called eccentric by most allegedly normal people, and like us, they would probably wonder why. This, I am told by psychologists, is the sign of a true eccentric, but what do they know about real life and real people? I like to consider myself a good judge of people and am full of confidence for Moondance and Zak's prospects. However, I have to admit that I find the accurate forecasting of which of our many correspondents will settle well on this side of the Channel a perennial problem.

Generally, a good rule of thumb is that I get it wrong and my wife gets it right. I believe it is something to do with women's intuition, while Donella says it is a matter of simple common sense, a faculty of which I am totally devoid.

There are, however, some general and broad categories into which various types of French property buyer or settler fit, and which have proved to give a fair indication of whether there is likely to be a happy outcome to the adventure.

The first category includes Lords of the Manor. These are people who buy property in France simply because it is so much cheaper than at home. They may not like the French or even France, and would much rather their place was in Surrey, but the nearest they can get to being landed gentry is by owning land and an impressive pile across the Channel. They are the sort of people who tell their friends that they own a chateau when what they have is really a biggish house with more than three bedrooms. Experience has shown that this type is not likely to make a go of their foreign adventuring, and are often people who know the price of everything and the value of nothing.

The second category in our rough guide includes Holiday Romantics. These sort of people are naïve enough to think that owning a property in France will be at least as much fun as their yearly three-week gîte holiday, with the added advantage that they will no longer have to pay an extortionate rental for staying there. They also persuade themselves that they will be able to cover the running costs, insurance, rates, travel expenses and even restoration costs by getting someone else to pay to take the place for a few weeks each summer. Unfortunately, they will soon discover that a couple of thousand other owners in their region have had the same good idea, and will actually end up letting friends use their

French home for free.

Our favourite and by far the most successful category consists of would-be settlers who either genuinely want to live in France, or in the countryside anywhere. They, like us, would never be able to afford even a modest country cottage in England, but can realise their hankering for rural life by adapting to their new circumstances.

So far, our settlers' guide has proved reasonably accurate when it comes to forecasting whether or not any particular person or couple will make a go of their hopes and dreams for a house or life in France. Life being what it is, there are always some notable exceptions, and that's what makes our little game such fun.

Of one thing we are sure. For the right sort of people, spending time in the countryside anywhere in France offers endless opportunities and rewards. A simple visit to a shop can be an adventure, and unblocking a sewage pipe on a frosty morning can put life into a perspective of almost staggering clarity.

Our last letter comes from a couple who are about to sign the final documents on a splendid village property in the Mayenne region. To raise the wind, they are selling their two-bedroomed terraced home in Portsmouth for twice the price of the classic *maison bourgeoise*, which has high iron railings, satisfyingly ornate and creaky gates, and comes complete with a guest cottage in the garden.

The husband in the happy partnership is a seafaring man, and the letter also clears up a mystery which has puzzled me for many years. When we last spoke on the telephone, I asked him why British sailors are often referred to as 'skates'. In a post-script to their letter, he tells me he has now done his research, and that the term comes from a common practice aboard 18th-century sailing ships. On a long sea journey, it was quite normal for the crew to catch a giant skate fish and nail it to the mainmast. The species, my correspondent assures me, has both male and female characteristics, and the latter are remarkably similar in size and shape to the human variety. Far away from dockside bawdy houses and lusting for a reminder of home, the crew would make regular recreational visits to the mast before the fish rotted away.

I shudder as I walk back to the mill cottage for breakfast. I don't know if the story is true or a typical example of coarse naval humour, but I shall certainly not be able to order skate with my chips at the *Donjon* restaurant for a very long time.

Close Encounters

No rain today so far, so I shall have a bath to celebrate.

This evening, we are dining with a couple of would-be settlers we met on the ferry boat, and I am looking forward to giving them some sound advice on the best way of realising their dream. Having said that, I will add the standard disclaimer that whatever course of action they take, I will not be held responsible for the outcome.

Jackie and Tom seem a sensible couple, excepting that they are eager to meet with René at some stage of their weekend in Cotentin. If they are not careful, he will sell them his cottage at a bargain price, which will not please the farmer who owns it. Our new friends introduced themselves while my wife and I were raiding the duty-free shop on a recent crossing, and Tom openly admits he was stalking us to see if we were who he thought we were. He had been reading my latest book when I shambled by en route to the shop, and he said it was extremely spooky to hear us discussing which economy size bottle of scotch we should buy for René.

Nowadays, it is unusual for us to make a crossing without being recognised and approached, and though I am often embarrassed by the encounters, Donella says I love the attention. She claims that I always walk around the entire ship at least five times during the voyage, and that she has caught me standing by the book department laughing helplessly at the contents of one of my books and recommending it to anyone who passes by. I say I am only trying to promote our on-board sales and bring a little colour into people's lives. I admit that there was an unfortunate incident when I approached a middle-aged woman who was looking at a Barbara Cartland autobiography and suggested she would find me much more interesting, but she was persuaded not to report me to the captain.

To prove to my wife that all the attention is not turning my head, I have offered to stay in our cabin for the whole journey, or wear a false beard when venturing out. My wife, however, says that as I already have a beard, I am obviously not serious in my claims to wish to travel incognito.

When a close encounter of the boat kind does happen, the ritual of recognition and approach invariably follows a set pattern, depending upon the circumstances and type of reader. Whatever the situation, the approach will always be made by a male. Sometimes it is the direct full-frontal attack, and in the past, I have been nabbed during a meal, while asleep, and even in the toilet. This can be embarrassing, especially if there are other passengers present. At other times, I will become aware of someone who has walked past me at least three times for no apparent good reason. Eventually, he will catch my eye, smile shyly or knowingly, then ask if I am indeed me. Occasionally, he will get my name right; more often he will ask if I am that fat bloke who made such a balls-up of buying a house in France.

The type of approach will also indicate the next stage, which will take one of three forms.

Sometimes, my reader will tell me how much he enjoys my work and go on to describe - sometimes in great detail and accompanied with notes, photographs and drawings - his own plans to buy a home in France. Sometimes, he will explain that he and his partner have already trod our path, and made a better or even worse fist of it. Always, he will say he found my writing much more or much less interesting and amusing than any other book on the subject.

Very rarely, I meet a real fan, and it is always disconcerting to encounter a stranger who knows so much about your life; especially when you have forgotten most of what you have written about.

Apart from our regular confrontations on the journey to and from La Puce, I occasionally meet a reader in the most unlikely circumstances, as happened during an arrival at our home in Portsmouth some years ago.

We were ferrying cases of wine, cider, cheese and other delicacies from the car when I noticed we were being keenly watched by a very large man at the top of a ladder resting against the house opposite. For a moment I wondered if he might be an undercover revenue spy, but on closer scrutiny decided against it. He was wearing typical building worker's summer rig of skimpy singlet and long shorts, sported a range of interesting tattoos, and had obviously practiced painting himself before starting on the house. In my experience, few Excise officers would have the initiative to create such an authentic disguise, and I reckoned that even the keenest would not bother to set up a special observation post for the sake of three bottles of moonshine Calvados. But he obviously found us interesting for some reason, and after absent-mindedly painting a window pane on the house next door, he gave me a hail.

'I know who you are, don't I?' he shouted, shaking his paintbrush triumphantly and pebble-dashing the house on the other side, 'that's Victor the Volvo, isn't it?'

Smiling smugly, I preened, shrugged deprecatingly at a passing traffic warden and waited for the revelation of my fame.

'I've read the books,' our distant admirer bellowed as he climbed down the ladder and crossed the road 'you're that Fred West, ain't you?'

After I told him that I was not a mass murderer and that my wife was the concrete-laying specialist of the family, he apologised for the mistake and told us he was the proud new owner of a farm in Normandy, and had found my books most entertaining and helpful.

Over a glass of cider in the office, Jimmy-John explained how he had bought the cottage, five acres and assorted outbuildings as the result of a slight misunderstanding. Having a weekend break driving around the Cherbourg peninsula with his wife, he had dropped in to a tourist bureau to ask about a bed and breakfast stop for the night. Unsurprisingly, none of the specially-trained staff spoke English, and Jimmy-John relied on sign language to indicate that they were looking for a house where they could sleep for the night. After much discussion with colleagues, the manager of the *syndicat d'initiative* made a couple of phone calls and replied with his hands and watch that the couple should return at seven that evening.

They did so, and were whisked away in the car of another non-English speaker. After travelling for an hour, they arrived in the gathering dusk at what appeared to be a derelict farmhouse. As Jimmy-John said, it was not a welcoming sight. Though used to the sometimes indifferent standards of French accommodation, he reckoned that glass in most of the windows should be a standard feature in any bed and breakfast enterprise, to say nothing of doors in the frames. Seeing his discomfiture, their guide called upon the translation services of an Englishman who lived nearby, and the confusion was cleared up. The farm was not on the tourist office books as a *chambre d' hôte*; it was on the books of the local estate agent as a property for sale. After accepting the profuse apologies of the agent and before getting back in the car, Jimmy idly asked the price of the ramshackle building. It was, he discovered, going for slightly less than the cost of a couple of weeks in Tenerife. As a builder and used to working on garages which would cost more than the dilapidated but characterful property, Jimmy thought about it for all of five minutes, looked at his wife for approval, and put in a bid.

It was accepted on the spot, and the couple who had gone to Cotentin for a weekend break had become homesteaders. Jimmy and his wife were now halfway through a crash course in French and a complete restoration of their new home, and loving every moment of their adventure. He still wasn't sure if the tourist office and his estate agent contact had really mistaken his request for a night's bed and breakfast, but he and his family were more than happy at the prospect of spending much, much more time in Cotentin than originally planned.

After hearing Jimmy-John's tale, we finished the bottle of cider to celebrate, opened the moonshine *calva*, and added his flag and details to the map of France in my office. Although Jimmy's farm is in our home region, he is very good company and it will be a delight to use his courtesy B&B facilities. Besides, as any French property owner knows, having a skilled, English-speaking builder on tap and just down the road is a real bonus.

Animal Crackers

Donella having prepared a gourmet meal for her menagerie, we are off to Bricquebec for a budget meal with our new friends, the would-be settlers.

Tonight, they will have the benefit of my first-hand experience on the subject of making a new life in Normandy. I, my wife says, will have the pleasure of talking non-stop for several hours. As I point out, she will at least have the pleasure of not having to listen as she has heard it all before.

Before we leave, I visit the attic of our mill cottage to collect forensic evidence of yet another non-paying guest. Climbing through the tiny hatch to the void above the bedroom, I see that the Mouse family have refurbished their quarters with the remnants of the lagging from the cold water pipes. They have also made a start on the covering to the electrical cables from the immersion heater. Investigating further, I recognise a fragment of the only copy of an important article I had been working on, and which I thought was safely locked away in my desk drawer. With the aid of my torch, I can see that their bijou little home behind the water tank is looking ever more comfortable, and even modish. Perhaps the mice have been watching the latest series of DIY programmes on our satellite television. So far, they have not actually stolen any of our furniture, and use the wallpaper from the landing for bedding rather than decorative purposes, but I shall know where to look if any more of my carpentry tools go missing.

When we first reconverted the cattle byre to its original function as a cottage, I set out on a campaign to rid the premises of all forms of wildlife, but my wife found the rat poison and made dark threats about adding some to my food if I did not get rid of it. From then on it was open house, with more species of animal and insect life to be found in the cottage than outside during the winter months. I know it sounds far-fetched, but I am sure that our beastly residents know they are welcome as far as my wife is concerned, and that she has the last word when it comes to visitors with more than two legs. I knew that I had lost the battle with the Mouse family when one of the younger members appeared while we were having an informal supper in front of the television. Not only did he clamber unconcernedly up on to the arm of my chair, but helped himself to a piece of camembert cheese before settling down alongside me to enjoy a programme on the Nature channel.

While I am, I think, indulgent towards my wife's unconditional love for all God's creatures, I drew the line last week when I found we have been sharing our bed with the winter feed store for our lone squirrel. Complaining of an unusual lump pressing against her when she awoke and discovering it was not any part of me, Donella got out of bed and found a hazel nut had somehow worked its way into her knickers. Further investigation found several more in her side of the bed, and a large pile in her part of the wardrobe. At first, I accused her of using them as bait to tempt the undernourished squirrel to take up residency, but she is obviously intrigued and delighted by the mystery. For some reason none of my clothes have been used for storage puposes, and the stupid creature has not thought to use the proper storage facilities in our larder. While I have so far tolerated the presence of other small furry creatures about the house, I shall have to do something about this latest development. I was reading an old copy of the *Daily Telegraph* recently, and saw a story about a squirrel ransacking an elderly couple's home while they were on holiday. According to the paper's wildlife pundit, it is not uncommon for squirrels to break into houses, and this one had caused thousands of pounds' worth of damage which the insurance company were refusing to cover.

Thinking about the situation as I sit in the attic, I make my plans to avert possible financial disaster and consider asking Freddo about his special recipe for squirrel with hazel nuts when we visit the Café de Paris this evening. I wish the creature no harm and we are probably stuck with him, but there is something grimly satisfying about the thought of using his own grocery supplies as a garnish.

* * * * *

My visit to the Mouse household has also created a new natural history mystery, and I have the tangible evidence of yet another squatter safely stowed away in a Tesco carrier bag. Over the years at La Puce, I have become something of an expert in animal excretions of all types, sizes and textures, but this sample is a real mystery. The stool I stumbled on in the attic of the mill cottage is solid and tubular and mottled black and white, and too big in my judgment for a rat, yet too small for an owl. Either the constant supply of high-energy food from Donella has caused the Mouse family to produce a monstrous new species, or we have geese in our loft. This I think unlikely, even for our household. I will take the sample to Bricquebec this evening and ask our friends for their expert opinions and conclusions.

A Night on the Town

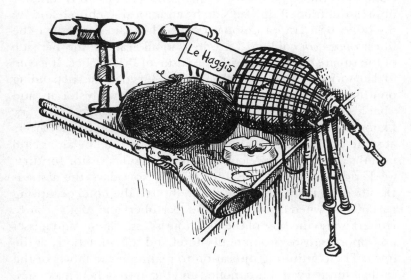

Le Haggis

We arrive at our favourite town, and park in what the locals claim to be the biggest market square in all France. It is certainly impressive, framed on one side by an imposing church and on the other by a Trappist monastery which is said to produce the finest *charcuterie* cold meat products in all France. Another side of the square is taken up with the castle of Bricquebec. It is said to date variously from the 11th, 12th or 13th centuries, depending on which of the locals is acting as unofficial town historian, and what historical figures he wishes to claim as past guests or owners. I know it is true that Rommel used the place as his headquarters at some time during World War II, but draw the line at fanciful notions about Queen Victoria being a regular visitor for dirty weekends with her ghillie John Brown. Nowadays, the castle is classified as an ancient monument, though the hotel occupying part of it is owned by our good friends Hubert and Albine Hardy. Hubert is also the boss of the local tourist association, and misses no opportunity to promote his hotel and the attractions of the town. The continuing operation to maintain the fabric of the castle is funded with Euro-money, and the town fathers make sure that Bricquebec gets its fair share of any grants going. There is always a team of local craftsmen working on some part of the building, and I am sure that some of the immaculate walls and towers have been painstakingly restored at least three times in the past year.

As we leave the car and walk across the square to meet our dinner companions at the Café de Paris, we hear what appears to be the screams of an animal in great pain. It is not a market day, and the dreadful noise appears to be coming directly from our local. I fleetingly wonder if Freddo the proprietor has taken to staging his regular hunting parties actually inside his bar to save the customers from having to venture out into the rain and cold of winter.

On our entry to the bar, the source of the din is resolved if not explained. Our local wide boy and very general dealer Didier is at centre stage, attempting to get a tune out of a set of Breton bagpipes. He is also wearing a plaid skirt. Thinking for a moment we have stumbled across a particularly weird Saturday evening fetish party, I then see a huge haggis on the bartop and realise that this is some sort of dress rehearsal for next month's Burns Night celebrations. Freddo the patron has joined in the spirit of the evening by wearing a paper tartan bonnet on his head, and has a large paint brush hanging from a string around his waist. After greetings are exchanged, our host confirms that he and Didier are testing the popularity of foreign theme nights, and that the occasion will also give him a chance to shift some of the Scotch whisky he has recently acquired from certain quarters. Looking around, I see that the regulars are watching the proceedings with typical Norman detachment, while our bemused new friends Jackie and Tom are being taught handy patois sayings and phrases by our latest exchange student, Ken Barnes.

A former master carpenter, Ken is approaching retirement age, and has taken advantage of one of the benefits of our twinning arrangement. Officially, Bricquebec is matched with the quaint and historic country town of Alresford in Hampshire. Unofficially, we have twinned the Café de Paris with our local pub in Portsmouth, and there have been several goodwill visits between the two establishments and their customers. After learning that he could buy a cottage in Bricquebec for about the same annual rent he pays for his terraced home in Hampshire, Ken is staying with a local family for a month while house-hunting, and I see he is already well on the way to going native. Being a thoughtful man with an enquiring and open mind and a liking for a smoke and drink, our friend fitted in well from the start of his visit, and has been taken to the community's heart. But before he arrived in Bricquebec, I cautioned him not to tell his new friends that his job for thirty years has been in the Portsmouth dockyard, using his skills to maintain the sails and spars of Nelson's flagship, HMS Victory. It is a curious fact that while the Cotentinese seem to bear no malice towards German visitors, they have long memories when it comes to more ancient encounters.

Before joining our friends, I have a word with Didier, who explains that he brought the haggis back from a recent business trip to Scotland, and has made it his business to educate the patrons of the Café de Paris on the traditions of the Burns ceremony, and the history and habits of the animal itself. Freddo has shown great interest in the idea of organising a hunting trip to the highlands of Scotland during the open season on the beast, but the regulars have been put off sampling the dish because of the presence of so many vegetables on the giant platter. Dider has responded by reminding them of France's traditional friendship and links with Scotland, and then there is the Norman connection. It is well documented, he assures his potential customers, that haggis herds once roamed free across the Cotentin landscape, and were introduced to Scotland by Bonnie Prince Arthur after one of his periodical flights to the peninsula during the English Civil War.

*   *   *   *   *

Finally reaching our table, I see that our new friend Tom is showing Ken a large plastic bottle with a name and some dates on the stopper. As he explains what it is, I realise that my wife and I are not the only couple who become entangled in strange and often bizarre incidents.

The bottle, Tom says, was given to him by an elderly friend who had heard about their visit to Normandy. Her husband, she said, had been involved in the evacuation at Dunkirk, and it had been his dying wish that his ashes be scattered on the surface of the English Channel. Though he had died and been cremated some twenty years before, his widow had a morbid fear of the sea, and the urn had remained on her mantlepiece ever since. Now that Tom was going to France, she had seen a way to redeem her promise to her husband. Would he be so kind as to tastefully empty the container over the side as the car ferry reached mid-Channel?

As Tom said, he could hardly refuse the request and duly went on deck during the crossing. Unfortunately, he was not a seafaring man, and had naturally chosen the side of the boat with the least people at the rail. It was only after emptying the container that he realised that the other passengers had sensibly chosen the sheltered side of the ferry. Rather than gently settling on the choppy waters of the Channel, the ashes of his friend's husband had immediately been blown inboard. Most had disappeared harmlessly in the general direction of the funnel, but a sprinkling had found their way on to an ice cream being enjoyed by a toddler standing nearby. He had bought the child another, said Tom, but had thought it best not to explain to the mother exactly what the gritty stuff was. Especially as the youngster had eaten a couple of mouthfuls before he could make amends.

We look at the empty bottle and reflect on the unpredictability of life and death, and my wife consoles Tom with the thought that the former sailor will now be able to cross and re-cross the Channel for all eternity, and totally free of charge.

To change the subject, I compliment Ken on his beret, and learn that he has already seen a most suitable retirement home. The tiny and dilapidated cottage is on the outskirts of Bricquebec and not officially on the market, but Ken's hosts say that an offer in excess of 30,000 francs may persuade the owner to part with it. As to property details, the important particulars are most encouraging. The cottage has a widow of an uncertain age living next door, and open fields as a neighbour on the other side. Even better, the distance to the Café de Paris has been timed as precisely six minutes at a gentle stroll. Apart from the developments with the cottage, Ken reports that he is making great progress with his French, and I take the opportunity to ask why he keeps calling out the name of a cartoon character as regulars leave the premises. He explains that I am obviously not as handy with the local lingo as I ought to be. As I should know, it is basic good manners to say 'see you later' when parting company with a friend. After another couple of puzzled regulars leave, I understand, and tactfully point out that the local way of saying cheerio is pronounced *plutar* as in 'later', and not Pluto as in Mickey Mouse.

*   *   *   *   *

As we talk and the Burns night rehearsal gathers momentum, we are joined by one of the handful of expatriots who have become fixtures in the town. BBC Charles is of an age with Ken, and like many English settlers with their own reasons for living anonymously abroad, he is an interesting and unusual character.

We first met in the nearby *Donjon* restaurant last year, when he heard my wife and I talking English and came over to introduce himself and point out the local tourist attractions. He was, he explained, a former foreign correspondent with the British Broadcasting Corporation, and was biding his time in Bricquebec till the terms of his pension and annuities were sorted out. For an hour or so he enthralled us with tales of his exploits in the Congo and other exotic locations, and then introduced us to his partner. A genuine Russian princess, the lady was a direct descendant of the Romanoff dynasty. We were disappointed to learn that Madame did not speak Russian, and later agreed that her huge sunglasses and flowing scarf made her look more like Biggles than the long-lost daughter of Anastasia, but she was a pleasant enough person. After accepting our invitation to join us for a bottle of wine, Charles told us all about a local celebrity who had written a book about the area, made a couple of million and retired to a water mill down the road. Such were his powers of oratory that it was not until we had left the restaurant some hours later that I realised he had, in fact, been talking about me. I had also been too entranced to notice that he had added his restaurant bill for the evening to ours.

From what Charles tells us as I stand him a couple of beers, his BBC pension has still not come through. Sadly, his princess has gone back to Mother Russia, and he is reduced to living in a cell at the Trappist monastery. As he touches me for a few francs until his cheque arrives from the BBC, he explains that his little room is quite comfortable, and his hosts are very kind. Being part of a silent order, however, conversation is not their strong point. On the plus side, the good brothers serve a liberal glass of wine after every devotional meeting, and there are no less than twelve a day.

If past form for his sort of expatriot adventurer is anything to go by, one day we will notice that Charles is not around, and learn from various debtors that he has moved on to quarters new or simply not woken up one morning. When that happens, we shall miss his engaging company, dry wit and fortitude, and our little community will be the poorer for his passing.

*　　*　　*　　*　　*

The Burns night is now in full swing, but I have had no luck in identifying our mystery resident. The carrier bag containing the animal droppings has been passed repeatedly around the bar, and everyone has passed an opinion on who or what is responsible for the contents. While admitting to not knowing what the animal could be, Freddo has offered to come to La Puce in the morning and shoot it. Carried away with the success of the evening, Didier has suggested it might be the mummified faeces of a long dead Cotentin haggis, and Young Pierrot has even taken the bag over to the *Donjon* and passed it around the tables. There was, he reports, keen interest from the diners but no conclusive agreement.

As the bag continues its round of new arrivals at the Café de Paris, I return from the toilets and note that we have been joined by our undercover police officer. Gilbert *le flic* has lived in the town all his life, went to school with every middle-aged resident of Bricquebec, and is seen by all the townspeople by day as he goes about his desk job at the local *gendarmerie*. By night, however, he disguises himself with a leather jacket and a change of parting, and haunts the nightspots of the town to observe any evil-doing and write down the names of those responsible. Freddo, however, says he is far from a harmless eccentric. His favourite trick is to drink with the locals then be waiting outside at closing time to invite drivers to blow into his *soufflé*, or breathalyser.

Pretending not to recognise the undercover detective, I nod coolly, rescue my carrier bag from a couple who are about to taste the evidence in the interest of solving our mystery, and retire to our table.

*   *   *   *   *

Much later, and the party crowd is thinning out. Outside the bar, the legendary Cotentin wind soughs through the vast square and chases departing revellers to their homes. Inside, the haggis has been eaten and pronounced surprisingly good. Didier has left after booking at least a dozen places on the hunting trip to Scotland, and we seem to be under special scrutiny from the undercover cop. I ignore him, order another round, and continue to enjoy a memorable evening in good company.

The talk now turns to my attempts to tell the world about our adventures in the Cotentin, and Jackie asks me why I choose to spend my life writing about this small corner of France. To begin with, I explain, it is far better than working for a living. I think everyone should write a book as long as there are enough trees to go round, and nobody has to buy or read them all. I'm glad that so many people seem to want to join us on our unimportant journey through life, and it is a delight as well as a privilege to be invited into my readers' minds to paint pictures of real life in real France. It is also a constant fascination to reflect that, at any time, someone far away is reading about our friends in Néhou. They may never have sought it and may not even particularly want it, but I am proud to have given them some small measure of acknowledgement - and even a sort of immortality.

As I warm to my theme, my wife tells me I am becoming maudlin and suggests we return to La Puce for a bedtime coffee and *calva*. We say goodnight to our host and Ken bids all the regulars *pluto*, then climb aboard Victor for the drive home. Turning back for a final farewell wave, I see through the window of the bar that Gilbert the undercover cop has crossed to our table and is investigating the contents of our abandoned Tesco carrier bag.

I think about returning for the bag or explaining to him what is inside, but decide against it. With any luck, the tireless sleuth will send the strange droppings to the Paris headquarters of the *Sureté* for analysis as a suspicious substance, and we will finally discover the identity of our mystery resident at La Puce.

Speaking in Tongues

Life is a foreign language: all men mispronounce it.

Christopher Morley
(American writer 1890-1957)

Shades of the skate story. I arrived at Madame Ghislaine's for the traditional Sunday morning *apéritif,* and was surprised to find René is not amongst the company.

When I asked after him, one of the customers explained that he was away fishing for ormers. I found this even more surprising, as I know this rare and highly-prized truffle of the sea is found mainly around the Channel Islands, and is only taken during spring tides.

After I innocently remarked that I did not know my friend was a diver, there was general and somewhat coarse laughter in the bar, and someone remarked that the Fox would not be getting even his feet wet, as he would be fishing for his ormers at low tide. Later, JayPay joined me on a visit to the *pissoir* alongside the grocery window and explained delicately that the remark about the delicious shellfish that we call the sea-ear or abalone was actually code for another sort of popular leisure activity. Though I have never seen one, the fleshy fruit inside the shell is said to look remarkably like a very private part of the female anatomy. My friend the Fox of Cotentin was, it seems, on a visit to the house of his accommodating friend, the Widow of Négreville.

JayPay also explained that, if René had been intending an encounter in the open air this fine morning, he would have been said to have been chasing lobsters in the gorse.

As we zipped up and returned to the bar, I wondered once again at the peculiarities of the *lingua franca*. All these ridiculous euphemisms and expressions seem a very strange kettle of fish to me.

* * * * *

It's all very well people going on about how disgraceful it is that so few Britons speak French and how everyone in France is fluent in our language, but in my experience, it just isn't true. Nobody in our village speaks a word of English, and I can't imagine them wanting to. In Bricquebec, our notary and bank manager pretend not to. We have long been aware of this tendency by certain sections of the French middle-classes to feign ignorance of our language when it suits them, but we can usually tell by their eyes when they are listening-in to our private conversations to see if they can gain some advantage. A good test is to say something outrageous about French food, driving, football teams or Napoleon, and watch to see if they blink.

Closer to home in our commune of Néhou, the locals not only ignore foreign languages, but also prefer their own patois to standard French. This puts visitors at a considerable disadvantage even if they are from another department of Normandy, or sometimes even another area of the Cotentin. Often, I have to offer my services as a translator, which does not go down well with the occasional French national who has difficulty communicating with a local, especially when they find out how bad my standard French is. Particularly afflicted by the problems of making themselves clearly understood tend to be the occasional government officials from St Lô on a mission to discover why the people of Néhou seem so incompetent at filling in tax returns and other official documents. Recently, I was present when one such visitor tried his hand at irony by suggesting our village go the whole hog and declare itself a separate republic. He was unaware that we have already looked into the pros and cons of separatism, with the Jolly Boys Club proposing that we approach Monaco with a request for tips on how best to go about the process of establishing a principality. The motion was eventually defeated when we got into a fractious debate about who was most entitled to take on the title of HRH of Néhou. Generally, the feeling about bureaucratic dictats and interference is that we get so little from a government that has done its best to destroy centuries of traditional (or as the politicians claim, inefficient) farming practices that we might as well go it alone. Apart, of course, from unemployment benefits, health and education services and other such basic communal rights.

A notable exception to the general language rule at Néhou is Didier, our local entrepreneur. Being a much-travelled and sophisticated businessman, he claims to have not only visited every part of England, but also to be fluent in the language and familiar with aspects of that most peculiar country. Much given to airing his knowledge of the latest overseas fads and fashions and developments, his dress code also reflects his knowledge of all things foreign. Today he is wearing a white suit with huge lapels which he claims to be all the rage in London, and is predicting that Mrs Thatcher will soon abdicate from her position in favour of Prince Charles. We have thought about enlightening him in the past, but don't want to embarrass a friend or threaten the regular supplies of English delicacies he allegedly buys from lorry-drivers in Cherbourg.

This morning it was our turn for a visit from Dodgy Didier's van. The Bar Ghislaine was packed with those wishing to find a real bargain, and the few who like to know what had been going on in the outside world. In full attendance today was the Néhou Jolly Boys Club, of which I have the honour to be an overseas member. Though having no written constitution or membership regulations, rules governing full entry to the club are very precise, and include having lived in or on the outskirts of the village since at least birth, having an above average consumption rate of alcohol, and an understanding of all things to do with the countryside and the nature and true meaning of life. And, of course, being free to attend at least five meetings every week. Another requirement is to be of an age when one has learned that just waking up each morning is a good start to the day. I am by far the youngest member, and our president is Old Pierrot. So far, I have not been able to discover exactly where he lives or how old he is, but it is whispered locally that he predates the village thanks to his secret elixir of life and special dietary regime, which seems to consist almost entirely of homebrew Calvados. I have also heard it claimed that he has magical powers and was on first-name terms with William the Conqueror. Whatever the truth about his age and mystic powers, Old Pierrot has become the Merlin to the court of the Jolly Boys Club, and hardly a meeting goes by without him making a mysterious prediction or pronouncement. Last week, he even put a curse on René Ribet for laughing at his yearly forecast of the worst flooding in living memory. It was the talk of the commune when René fell off his moped and broke his wrist on the way home from the meeting. The more superstitious of the villagers credited Old Pierrot's black arts with the accident, but I think it more likely that Mr Johnny Walker was to blame.

Apart from such entertaining diversions, pure philosophy reigns during our sessions at the Bar Ghislaine. I can think of few pleasures which surpass a gathering of the Jolly Boys Club on a wet winter afternoon in the Bar Ghislaine, with the single log in the grate at least smouldering, a bottle of *calva* on the table, and our minds ablaze with the possibilities of restructuring the world and its ways. It is often difficult for me to follow the threads of argument, but I find our region's homebrew apple brandy has almost miraculous powers in aiding my powers of concentration. Since being given the honour of becoming the first outsider admitted to the ranks of the JBC, I have occasionally tried to introduce refinements to the rules, such as other members buying the occasional round, but my motions have been rejected without a vote. Membership of women even as associate members is, of course, unthinkable.

Today, other members present included JayPay the chef, Old Pierrot, Marcel Bernard and, of course, René Ribet. But the main event today was Didier's weekly visit. From the latest scandal to rock our rival village of St Jacques de Néhou to the less important but equally salacious details of goings-on abroad, he was as ever able and eager to keep us informed.

Today, he has been telling his audience about recent events at the White House, and the locals are amazed that the President of the United States could be in trouble for making full use of his most important parts. In France, naturally, he would be given a citation rather than a trial.

It was then time for the traditional story-telling session, when Didier brings us the latest jokes from home and abroad. He began with the topical tale of President Clinton's excuse that he actually asked Monica Lewinsky to sack his cook and she misheard him, but it fell rather flat as the play on words does not work in French, let alone patois.

As the meeting broke up and Didier prepared to set off for his next appointment, I asked him about an anecdote regarding a shellfish and a mole he had told earlier. To the best of my memory, I will quote the actual exchange as I believe it gives a fair example of the communication difficulties any settler in France experiences from time to time:

Me: So what was all that about a mole and a mollusc, Didier?

Him: I was explaining how I came to be given the name of Mr Mole when I was in the Secret Service.

Me: You mean because you were an undercover agent?

Him: No, I mean because I was up all night at clubs and bars. By morning you could hardly see my eyes.

Me:	So they called you Mr Mole because you had, as we say, eyes like rainholes in the snow.
Him:	Exactly. Only we prefer to say that someone has eyes like a winkle's whole arse.
Me:	Ah, you mean a winkle's arsehole?
Him *(irritably):*	No, I mean a winkle's whole arse.
Me *(desperately):*	But you see, the whole point of the joke is surely that tiny eyes look just like a winkle's backside?
Him *(sharply):*	Have you ever seen a winkle's whole arse?
Me *(grudgingly):*	No.
Him *(triumphantly):*	Well, there you are then…

*   *   *   *   *

Apart from these occasional confusions over common usage, one thing all my French friends are agreed upon is their opinion of my standard French. The sound of me speaking their precious language, as one rather unkindly put it, is enough to make any true Frenchman wish he was deaf.

Regardless or perhaps because of this attitude, many French people still take every opportunity to pretend they don't know what I am talking about, even when they patently do. I have written before about this peculiar and irritating trait, experienced on my early visits to France. But it still happens, even nowadays. Only recently, I used my best French to ask the posh Parisian wife of a friend if we were now friendly enough for me to give her a kiss each time we met, and he appeared horrified. Later, he told me that while he accepted that the French - and especially those from Paris - do not have the repressed Victorian attitude to sex so common in England, it was nevertheless quite unacceptable to propose to his wife that I shag her on a regular basis. At least, he said, it was extremely bad manners to make the proposal in his presence.

After consulting my dictionary, I pointed out that it was not my fault that the French should choose exactly the same word for fuck as for kiss, with the meaning changing dependent upon context or the fine tuning of pronunciation. Anyway, what he doesn't know is that his wife phoned me for weeks afterwards to tell me when he was away on business, so I don't think she had any problem with getting what she thought was my drift.

*   *   *   *   *

Another typical example of misinterpretation arrived today with our weekly communiqué from Moondance and Zak, who report that they are settling down really well in their new home in Mayenne. This is quite a relief, as Moondance likes cuddly animals, is a strict vegetarian, and only found out on moving-in day that their neighbour is a veal farmer. Apart from the bloodstained clothing, she says, he seems to be quite a friendly man and wants to make them feel part of the community. They have, however, politely refused his offer to go with him to the local abattoir for a day out.

In their fax, our post-hippie friends also say that they have been having some communication problems with their other neighbour, a man who lives alone and speaks his own version of patois that cannot be understood by even the local people. When they first moved in and invited him over for a drink, virtually the whole evening was spent in achieving the exchange of names. As they got to know him, he became more friendly and set about advising them on the ways of the countryside, including an often-repeated warning about the problems of finding crap in their shoes in the morning. At first thinking he was warning them of the nocturnal habits of his cat, our friends would carefully put their footwear on top of the wardrobe before going to bed. After a particularly enjoyable evening entertaining friends, however, they forgot the routine. The confusion over the mystery shoe-shitter was solved next morning when they found a large brown toad, or *crapaud*, snoozing contentedly in Moondance's left slipper.

*   *   *   *   *

My personal problems with getting by in a foreign language are also compounded by the fact that I am slightly deaf in one ear, and most days have to filter any incoming sounds through a constant buzzing. My wife says that I am imagining it and rely on the tinitus excuse when I don't want to hear something she says, but the doctor tells me my condition is the result of abusing my hearing when I worked at a commercial radio station. This period of my life taught me a lot about communications, and especially the problems that can arise through the simple act of conversation.

As part of my duties as a producer of phone-in programmes, I would sit in the control room and feed calls through to the on-air presenter, and also set up and play in the musical breaks between calls. One of the problems of taking live phone-ins is the threat of crank callers, who take a delight in throwing a spanner into the smooth-running of the programme. Sometimes, like naughty children, they just want to shock listeners by letting rip with a few obscenities. Others are more devious, and delight in causing chaos. The trick for the producer lays in the initial screening, which is done by having a few words with the caller before he or she is put on air. In those few moments you have to judge whether the next contributor is going to be articulate or hesistant, controversial, defamatory, obscene or just plain boring.

On the morning in question, I was nursing a hangover from the previous night's radio roadshow, but was still being careful to check that all calls through to the presenter were carefully monitored. This was important because she was new to the job, and very nervous. I had taken her through her period of training, and promised her I would personally handle every technical aspect of the programme, from selecting and playing in the records to sorting out and airing the recorded commercial breaks. I had also deliberately picked the innocuous subject of holiday memories as the main theme of the programme, and all seemed to be going well when I piped through a call from a young man who wanted to talk about his recent holiday trip to Austria.

'How naice,' commented my presenter, who was by now beginning to relax , 'and did you have a lovely time?'

'Not really,' replied the caller quite casually, 'while I was there I fell in front of a train. It cut my legs off.'

There followed a long moment of frozen silence as the presenter went in to blind panic mode. Then she looked up from her desk and our eyes met through the glass screen. It was decision time, and the options were clear. If we took the call as a hoax and I disconnected him, it would make her appear heartless. If it was a wind-up merchant, the situation could only get worse. Thinking quickly, I made the sign for her to get rid of him as gracefully as possible and introduce some music. My new presenter took a deep breath, opened her mouth and promptly completely forgot the first rule of broadcasting, which is to always engage brain before speaking: 'Oh dear, how terrible for you,' she wittered, 'I hope it didn't spoil your holiday too much. This next tune is just for you, and I hope it cheers you up.'

As the duty engineer collapsed on the floor in helpless laughter, I pressed the button to play the next record and realised just too late the title of the song I had chosen to fill this musical break. It was a popular golden oldie by a chap called Andy Fairweather-Lowe, and the name of his one big hit was *Wide Eyed and Legless*.

Selling Out

Monday morning and a treat is in store. Today we shall make our weekly visit to the market at Bricquebec. As if to mark the occasion it even stopped raining for ten minutes earlier today, which means Old Pierrot's prediction may yet be proved wrong.

Before making ready for our trip to town, we venture into the mill garden, and stand beside the thundering cascade to look out across the flooded water meadow. It is certainly living up to its official name of *le reservoir*, and the big pond is getting bigger by the day. Donella expresses concern about the wellbeing of the fish, and I ask if she is worried they may drown in the constant downpour. She is not amused by what she calls my callous remark, and says that if the big pond continues to overflow, Psycho and his tribe could be washed into the neighbouring fields. I see her point, and make a mental note to warn the local farmers to move their livestock to higher ground if the flooding worsens. I have heard that the deadly Amazonian piranha fish can strip a fully-grown horse to the bone in twenty minutes, but I bet Psycho and his chums could do it in half the time.

Before returning to the cottage to put on our going-to-market clothes, we sit on the bench and look at the cascade, and I wonder rather smugly just how many people can boast of a waterfall in their back garden. In an idle moment, I once calculated that around a million gallons of mostly fresh water crash down into the basin every eight hours during the rainy season. It seems an awful waste that it all just rushes out to the sea at Carentan, and I begin to muse on the commercial possibilities of harnessing this prodigious power. Then I remember our disastrous attempts to bottle and sell the water from our well, and suggest we set off for market. Before we reach the cottage, there is a mournful squawk from the direction of the big pond, and my wife says she must remember to buy another case of sardines in town. Obviously, she has forgotten that I am not supposed to know about her secret trysts with our overfed heron.

*   *   *   *   *

Arriving in the square at Bricquebec, we receive the predictable black looks from a huddle of small men in big boots. Civilians are not particularly welcome when the farmers gather to conduct what they see as the real business of the day. Hard bargaining is the norm at any traditional animal marketplace, but here the Cotentinese farmers take every centime made or lost on a deal very seriously indeed. Allegedly, the damp red patches found dotted about the square are not always the result of an unfortunate animal being despatched on the spot for easier transportation purposes. This occasional bloodletting is the main reason we always arrive after the animals have gone and the stallholders have descended on the square. It's not that Donella would be frightened by the sight of a punch-up, but I fear for the safety of anyone she might think is mistreating an animal.

An hour passes as the ancient paving slabs are hosed down, the pens and cages removed and the farmers depart to the various bars where they will celebrate or mourn their morning's work. Already, the square is filling up with dozens of stands and stalls in various stages of assembly, and we wander amongst them to enjoy the atmosphere. We find all markets fascinating; ours is one of the largest and liveliest on the peninsula, and hardly a soul from the surrounding villages and hamlets will miss the traditional start to the week. When we first arrived in the Cotentin, we could not understand the popularity of the markets, as most of the food produce on sale could be bought much cheaper from supermarkets or even in the nearby shops. It was not until we settled in a fairly remote area and got into the rhythm and pace of country living that we realised the real significance of any rural market. After a week spent working in relative and sometimes complete solitude, the soul cries out for a regular opportunity to rub shoulders with other human beings instead of livestock. Companionship by proximity is the real reason country people go to market. At least, that's my view. My wife says it is actually because visitors can get a whole week's worth of gossip in one glorious hit, and it is certainly true that as much tittle-tattle as money is exchanged at Bricquebec market. Whatever the reason for the gathering, the traders are all busily setting out their stalls for their weekly bonanza, and their enthusiasm is infectious. I would rather be at a Norman market than any air-conditioned shopping mall or precinct in Britain.

We take our time in strolling through the lines of stalls, and I divert Donella's attention from a row of crates containing some very unhappy-looking turkeys. Alongside, a small man is cooking up a pot of Vietnamese delicacies, and beside him a giant Moroccan is touting a range of exotic leatherwear that I cannot see suiting the tastes or shapes of the average Cotentinese housewife. Also gearing up for business are the owners of the mobile shops selling sweets, cheeses, meat and a hundred shapes, textures and flavours of bread, and there are at least a dozen stands offering the local equivalent of hot dogs. The spicey *merguez* sausages are more than delicious on a cold December morning and when eaten in a crisp *baguette* with lashings of Dijon mustard and a huge portion of chips. Other snacks include the French version of Welsh Rarebit and very un-Italian pizzas, filled pancakes and giant mugs of thick Normandy potato and cream soup. Nearby, whole ducks, chickens and joints of lamb and beef are sizzling on mechanical turnspits above oaken logs. Wafting across the square, the combined aroma of these delights is irresistible, and we do not resist. Munching on a hot sandwich of goat's cheese and olives, I drag my wife away from a stall selling chain saws and try to interest her in something less expensive as a souvenir of our day at market.

Later, we take a break for coffee, and decide to venture into the lair of Madame Lefarge. There are a dozen bars in Bricquebec, each catering for a particular type of clientele, but the proprietor of the *Café Bon Accueil* appears to cater for none. A large and intimidating woman with a small and understandably nervous husband, she bears down on those who dare trespass on her territory like a galleon in full sail. If she eventually approves of you and your manner and dress code, it is possible she may take your order. Madame obviously considers customers as an inconvenient interruption to her daily duties of haranguing her husband. Every other bar in Bricquebec will be packed this morning, with farmers trying to get their bulbous Norman noses into tiny glasses of liqueur, and housewives resting from their bargaining encounters with the stallholders. But here, we will find no problem in getting a seat, providing we pass the threshhold audition. As we walk across the square, I see that the patch outside the Lefarge lair is once again occupied by the least successful traders. Whether this is because the market manager places them there deliberately as a sort of punishment, I do not know, but today is no exception. Approaching the darkened bar, I am amazed to see a woman actually trying to sell mistletoe. Even more astonishingly, she is not a new English settler with what she thinks is a bright idea. In an area where the plant grows like weed and farmers will almost pay you to take it away, the obviously dejected local trader must be either doing it for a bet, or be employed by Madame Lefarge to frighten prospective customers away.

Another trader not having much luck is a solitary figure standing beside a table bearing a pile of religious tracts. As we pass, I nod sympathetically, and my wife gives me a sharp dig in the ribs. She is obviously warning me against encouraging an appeal from the lone missionary. As I know, it is not that she does not want to hear his message, but that she does not want to expose him to a session with me. Our house in Portsmouth is said to be the only location in the city where Jehovah's witnesses cross the road as they pass, and Donella claims I am the only person she has ever seen pursue an opinion pollster to insist on giving my opinion. It is true that when people with something to sell arrive at our door, I tend to invite them in rather than slam the door in their faces or hide behind the sofa till they give up and go away. I have noticed that the invitation to come in for a nice chat tends to put them very much on the defensive. It is even alleged in our neighbourhood that I am on the blacklist for calls from double glazing salesmen, though the front of our home in Portsmouth makes it obvious we are very much in the market for their products.

In spite of Donella's warning, I stop and speak to the man and find that he is an English settler. We had not heard of or met him before as he lives in our rival village of St Jacques de Néhou, but he seems a decent chap in spite of that.

We - or rather I - spend a pleasant few minutes talking to the lonely missionary, who explains that he came over to do good works by signing up as many local people as possible to the Protestant religion. I do not comment, but suspect that this would be a bit like going to Baghdad to sell bibles. The lanes and byways of Cotentin are plentifully sprinkled with roadside shrines, and virtually everyone we know subscribes to Catholicism, whether or not they practice what is preached every Sunday in every village church. But we wish him luck in his mission anyway. We also try to persuade him to join us for a coffee, but he is adamant that he will not leave his post in case he misses a possible convert. I think he will have a long wait, but admire him for his enthusiasm, and wish I had his sort of conviction.

*   *   *   *   *

Inside the Good Welcome Café we are met by the formidable Madame Lefarge, who listens to our application for a brace of coffees with Calvados, then grudgingly sweeps off to shout the order at her husband, even though he is only a yard away on the other side of the counter.

Choosing seats by the window, we enjoy the activity outside, then take stock of our fellow customers. They do not occupy our attention for long, as there are only two. Both male and with the pained expression of those who think that life is playing a trick on them, they sit in utter silence opposite each other, taking occasional and tentative sips from their coffee cups as if they were tasters in Lucrezia Borgia's research laboratory. Like Madame's husband, both men are small and clearly aged beyond their years. In a whisper, I ask Donella why she thinks they come to such a place, and she says they probably feel at home here.

Our drinks arrive, and Madame Lefarge towers over me till I produce the necessary coins. She does not actually spit in our coffee, but it is obvious that she would rather we took our custom elsewhere, which is another reason my wife likes to come here. We first visited the Good Welcome when on an introductory pub crawl of Bricquebec with René Ribet, and immediately got off to a bad start with the proprietor. Before we entered, René told me that it would tickle Madame if I used the patois when ordering Donella's coffee, and the correct term would be *jus de chausettes*. After her husband had ducked beneath the bar and Madame had retreated to her private quarters to recover from the insult, our new friend explained that I had asked for a cup of her best sock juice. To be fair though, I do not think we are being singled out for special treatment on our visits to the bar. As we have seen over the years, Madame treats all her customers just as badly.

After watching the bustle of activity beyond the window, I look around and wonder yet again why all Norman bars are, in essence, the same bar. The floors are always tiled like a public toilet, and the walls always seem to bear the same shade of dead fish wallpaper. There will always be too much window and not enough wood, and what there is will have its natural grain and hue hidden beneath layers of custard yellow paint. As I have said before, we love virtually everything about our adopted homeland, but there are some British institutions, products and establishments that we sorely miss, and a proper English pub comes high on the list. Especially when sitting in the Good Welcome Cafe.

Portable luxuries like hard cheese and proper baked beans can always be brought over from England, and the *Daily Telegraph* is available at Cherbourg ferryport, but nobody has as yet seen the value of shipping an Indian restaurant or British pub lock, stock and barrel across the Channel. There is a pale imitation called rather unimaginatively The English Pub in Octeville, but the atmosphere is just not the same as the owners have inevitably adapted it to suit French tastes. There is a sit-down meal and a cabaret on Saturday evenings, and there has not been a traditional English Friday night punch-up since the place opened. Our friends Mike and Rita seem to be doing surprisingly well with their Anglo-French pub and restaurant on the coast, however, and we shall drop in to see them on our way back from Brittany next month.

Now, we finish our coffee and *calva*, nod goodbye to the other customers, and thank Monsieur Lefarge for his hospitality. Although Madame is elsewhere, he does not reply, and averts his eyes in case she appears like the wicked witch in a pantomine and catches him fraternising with the enemy.

*   *   *   *   *

Outside in the square, business at the weekly market has reached its peak, and we see that Alan and Sally Offord are doing a roaring trade. This is a huge credit to their entrepreneurial skills and judgment of what British foodstuffs the French can be tempted to buy, as so many settlers have tried and failed their hand at this form of niche marketeering. The number of normally dour Norman farmers we have seen self-consciously wearing Father Christmas hats and masks this morning is further evidence of the couple's trading skills, and I think again about the attractions of taking a stall at the weekly Bricquebec fair. The idea of knocking out goods for real cash in such a characterful setting has immense appeal, but Donella thinks my idea of selling our books to the French would not be a winner. Apart from hardly any of the potential customers being able to read English, she says they would not have the slightest interest in what I have to say about them and their surroundings. I have suggested that we look at the practicalities of bringing out a French language version of my works, but she says I would have trouble in successfully translating a Janet and John book. My idea for a market stall may have to be put on the back burner for the moment, but I am sure we can make a go of it if we get the product right.

As we approach our friends' busy stall, I see further evidence of how deep-rooted is the French antipathy to all things foreign, and especially English. A woman with the sort of face that encourages mothers to check that their children are safely indoors is scowling suspiciously at the goods on the Offord stall. As we watch, she looks round, then reaches out hesitantly for a free sample of Sally's home-made manor cake. After a moment of handling the slice as if it were a particularly unstable piece of plastic explosive, she lifts it to her nose and sniffs loudly. The frown turns to a look of surprise, and for a moment I think she will actually taste it, but prudence and prejudice prevail. The woman carefully replaces the cake, picks up and pays for a jar of Branston pickle, then hides it at the bottom of her shopping basket before scurrying away like a customer leaving a dirty book shop.

We spend a few pleasant minutes with Sally and Alan, and in between customers, they tell us about their progress in bringing a taste of Britain to the Cotentin. Apart from the Branston pickle, a very popular line at the moment is jars of humble sandwich spread. Apparently, it is all the rage in Paris, with hostesses putting dollops in silver salvers for use as a *chic* salad side dish, and Sally makes me promise not to spread the word about its relatively low status in England to our more sophisticated French friends.

It's time to return to La Puce, and walking back to the car I comment on the general merriment my Father Christmas mask is occasioning. My wife gently reminds me that anyone less in need of a disguise to look like a fat man with a white beard would be hard to imagine.

Wet, Wet, Wet

It is still raining. We have not ventured out for days, and I am worried about the integrity of our 18th-century roof. I made a return visit to the loft today and was relieved to see that the Mouse family has made a workmanlike job of repairing a particularly bad leak above their quarters. They used a couple of pages from the manuscript of my latest book as caulking, but I have a spare copy, so all is not lost.

When we restored the mill cottage the roof was leaking like a sieve. We did not want to replace the original terra cotta tiles with bland modern slate, so called René Ribet in to see what he could do. As the most skilled roofer in the region, he said, it would be possible for him to carefully remove the whole roof, then put back and realign every slate. At the same time he would seal up all the gaps. It would take him much longer than simply whipping a new *couverture* on, and therefore cost a little more. But when he finished, it would look as good as new, or rather old. The restored roof, he assured us, would then be as tight and dry as a duck's back passage. I told him to go ahead, but was worried to see that he scorned what he said was the modern, costly and uneccesary practice of lining the roof with waterproof felting material, and had simply taken all the tiles off then put them back again in roughly the same order. At least, he said that is what he had done when we came back from a visit to England and were presented with his bill. I thought it strange that all the moss and other growths on the roof seemed to be in exactly the same position as before, but René said that was the really hard part of the operation, and how pleased he was that I had noticed how skilful he had been in making it look as if the roof had not been touched for centuries. All this alleged surgery took place in the relatively dry season, and it is only since my visit to the loft that I have discovered that the roof is still leaking badly, and that daylight still shows through the gaps between the tiles.

With a bit of luck, the weather will break soon and the ground will have a chance to recover, but all the auguries are bad, and the impending disaster is now the main topic of conversation at the Jolly Boys' meetings. Older members are talking with grim relish about the winter that the *val de Néhou* was declared a disaster area, and Didier is taking bets on how many cows will be drowned. It has not helped the general mood of doom that the local carpenter recently started work on a redundant fishing boat he took in settlement of a bad debt, and some wag sneaked into his yard one night with a pot of paint and re-named it The Ark of Néhou.

Even if the rain stops soon, I fear that the clay soil of La Puce will take a long time to drain off. This morning, I looked out of the back bedroom window and saw that the big pond has now joined the little pond and the water meadow has become one huge lake. My wife continues to worry about the residents of both ponds, but I cheer her up her by pointing out that now they have so much more space, the incidents of violence between the Cray gang and Psycho the goldfish and his tribe should hopefully diminish.

Although I am striving to treat the threat of flooding lightly, I am quite worried about what may happen if the water reaches and covers the stone wall dividing the mill garden from the water meadow. On our side of the wall, it is all down hill to the cottage. When the lord of the manor chose the site for and built the Mill of the Flea all those years ago, he spared no effort or expense to ensure that the water would go past the buildings, but he could not have envisaged these conditions.

Climate and prevailing weather patterns in France is a subject with which many English settlers have a problem, as their perception is usually based upon their own limited experience at home and abroad. Most people base their ideas on a touchingly simple calculation that France is further south than Britain, so the weather must be generally better wherever you are. They also seem to think that for every mile one goes due south from the Channel, the warmer it will get. This is, of course, not true, as anyone who has experienced a winter in Provence will confirm.

In fact, the micro-climate in Cotentin is virtually the same as it is in southern England, and just a degree or so hotter in summer and colder in the winter. As we are on a peninsula, it also rains often. Being mostly from the town and used to having central heating in their houses and pavements under their feet, English people are shielded from the effects of the weather, and many of our visitors seem to think that it is our fault when the skies open, and that mud is an avoidable inconvenience caused by our sloppy land management. They also seem to think that our winter dress code is based upon eccentricity rather than experience, though soon learn the truth about living in the countryside when they arrive in unsuitable clothing. Last winter, a trendy reporter from a posh woman's magazine turned up to do a piece about the delights of living a sophisticated rural life in a restored Normandy mill. Despite our advice on sensible footwear, she arrived wearing white stiletto heeled shoes, and one of them inevitably went missing when she took a gentle stroll in the spongy area around the septic tank. I explained about the cracked sewage pipe and offered to root around for her shoe, but she said not to bother. Our PR exercise was all a waste of time anyway, as the proposed article never appeared.

*   *   *   *   *

Now I have seen it all.

This morning, I squelched into the cottage to find a large lizard taking its ease on a rug in front of the stove. Even my wife draws the line at inviting serpents into our home, so I can only conclude that it is sheltering from the incessant rain. Tomorrow, I shall ring the carpenter at Néhou and ask if his ark is up for sale.

Friends and Neighbours

A986 ROT

Beechwood fires burn bright and clear,
If the logs are kept a year.
Store your beech for Xmastide,
With new cut holly laid beside.
Chestnut's only good they say,
If for years it's stored away.
Birch and firwood burn too fast,
Blaze too bright and do not last.
Flames from larch will shoot up high,
Dangerously the sparks will fly.
But ashwood green and ashwood brown,
Are fit for a queen with golden crown.
Oaken logs if dry and old
Keep away the winter's cold.
Poplar gives a bitter smoke,
Fills your eyes and makes you choke.
Elmwood burns like churchyard mould
E'en the very flames are cold.
Applewood will scent the room,
Pearwood smells like flowers in bloom.
But ashwood wet and ashwood dry,
A king may warm his slippers by.

In spite of the weather, or perhaps because of it, we have decided to go on a foraging expedition. Due to the amount of time we have been spending indoors, the wood stove has been eating into our fuel reserves, and the log pile behind the cottage is getting uncomfortably low. The good news is that Donella has spotted a new and ready-made supply of fuel in one of the top fields, and we must harvest it before someone else does. Another bonus is that if the worst does happen and the floods arrive, we can always lash the biggest of these mystery logs together and make a raft for emergency use. We climb into our waterproof gear, collect an axe and saw from the shed, and set out on our hunter-gathering expedition in high spirits. The arrival of a bonus pile of kingly ash is good news indeed.

In an area where most homes are heated by log-burning stoves, the value placed on quality firewood cannot be overestimated. To our Norman neighbours, a tree is valued not so much for its beauty as its worth when cut down and chopped into stove-sized logs, and I have to admit that we are beginning to adopt this mentality. With a mature tree providing enough fuel for cooking and heating for the best part of a winter, it has become increasingly easy to look at a stately oak and see only a hundred hot dinners in every bough. And La Puce is a veritable treasure-trove of fuel. Due to neglect over the years, our roadside copse is littered with fallen trees. Age, storms, infestation and the odd badly-driven tractor regularly provide new corpses for us to feed upon. Last autumn, a giant beech came crashing down in Hunter's Walk after a gale, and we fell upon the carcass before the leaves stopped quivering.

Today it appears that we have a gift from an unusually conscientious neighbour rather than the elements. While badger-spotting in the larger of the roadside fields yesterday, my wife discovered a huge pile of neatly trimmed and stacked logs alongside the hedge marking the boundary of our land. Investigating further, she saw that severe surgery had taken place on a sturdy ash tree growing on our side of the hedge, and a ladder was still resting against the trunk. All the branches had been lopped off, and there was another, even larger pile of logs on our neighbour's terrain. Obviously, my wife said, Old Mr Moineau had been at work, and had left the branches on our side of the hedge as our fair share. While agreeing that the appearance of a pile of free and already butchered wood was warming news, I have my doubts that our benefactor is Mr Moineau. He must be over ninety years of age, and even in Cotentin this is a good age to be shinning up trees with a chain saw. Besides, we have not seen him for several years, and this is quite a space between sightings. Another thing that visitors and settlers find hard to accept about the way of life in our area, and for all I know, throughout rural France, is that people like to keep themselves to themselves, especially if they live relatively cheek-by-jowl. It is not just in over-populated towns and cities where boundary disputes can arise, and neighbours in the countryside generally have much more to fall out about. With his ramshackle roadside cottage no more than a quarter of a mile from our house as the crow flies, Mr Moineau is our closest neighbour, and he seems to think we are too close for comfort. When we first arrived at La Puce, we called at his home several times, but he was either out or pretending to be, and our friends in the village say he is not a great one for visitors or social niceties. Like most reclusive people, he is the centre of much conjecture, and said to be enormously rich, spending all his time counting his fortune in the cellar. I don't know if this is true, but he has certainly not wasted any money on DIY in the past half-century or so.

*　　*　　*　　*　　*

As we are anticipating a good haul of logs, we decide to take the car, so I go to tell Victor he is on tractor duty today.

Of all the cars we have ever owned, Victor has been the most versatile and valuable. Over the years, he has helped us ship many tons of goods across the Channel, and is now in semi-retirement at La Puce. I read somewhere that more than seventy per cent of all Volvos are still on the road, and Victor has certainly left a good percentage of his bodywork and bits on the highways and byeways of Cotentin. 'It's not expensive when you consider what goes into it' was the current Volvo slogan when Victor was born, and I think the advertising people who dreamed up that slogan would be amazed if they knew what he had carried since joining the family. Nowadays, though, he is beginning to show his age, and his duties are restricted to taking us on relatively short journeys, or working on the land. I know that one day he will either conk out in the middle of a field or simply refuse to wake up on a chilly morning, and that will be the best way for him to go. We have already discussed a suitable use for his remains, and I favour the pragmatic approach of our friends in Néhou, who find that dead cars make ideal chicken coops. My wife refuses to contemplate the thought, and has been talking about a dignified burial in the water meadow. I think she is over-reacting, but at least this would be less costly than her original idea of staging a Scandinavian warrior's farewell, with Victor drifting into the sunset off Utah beach on a fire-raft.

*   *   *   *   *

Fortunately, Victor appears in good health and spirits despite the constant deluge, and we are soon lurching up the cart track towards the road which runs alongside La Puce. We park alongside a convenient hole in our roadside hedge and climb through to investigate the situation. Just as Donella has described, the newly-shorn ash marks the spot, and the huge pile of logs is resting safely on our side of the hedge marking the boundaries of our terrain.

For the next hour we drag logs from the pile across the field, through the hole in the hedge and on to Victor's roof rack. Occasionally, a car screams by with a wail of protest at our position just around a dangerous bend in the road, and I have some good practice at verbal and visual insults. Donella is by now worried about the size and weight of the load, and points out that Victor's back bumper is almost touching the ground. But the fever is on me, and I insist we can clear the pile. Dusk is gathering, the rain is falling even harder, but I want to be sure that we collect every scrap of firewood rather than leave it to a passing predator. Our activities will have been seen by motorists on the way to St-Sauveur-le-Vicomte, and even now the word about our valuable and isolated log pile will be spreading through the seamier bars and dives.

Finally, the last log has been eased on to the giant pile aboard the roof rack, and we are ready for the return journey to the mill cottage. After another inspection of the springs, I suggest that Donella drives, while I walk behind the car to pick up any flotsam and to enjoy further sport with passing motorists. We are about to set off, when a small car rounds the bend and screeches to a halt alongside. A stocky individual of around my age jumps out and approaches us with much stylised arm-waving. At first I think he wants to buy some logs from us, and then I realise that he is very unhappy, and claiming that they are all his.

Eventually, when he has calmed down a little and spotted that I am carrying a felling axe, he identifies himself as the son of Mr Moineau. His father is hardly cold in his grave, he says, and here we are plundering his possessions like thieves in the night. As the eldest son, he is the rightful owner of every log, faggot, branch and twig that we are stealing, and he will help us move them from our car to his. Now. It is now my turn, and while sympathising with his loss, I point out that the logs in question have come from my tree, which is growing in my field on my land, and are now destined to travel on my car to my log pile, and from there to my stove to heat my home and cook my dinners. Furthermore, I could bring into question his rights in laying claim to the logs on his side of the hedge, and the ladder against our tree shows that he has clearly been trespassing on our land. In the sad circumstances, however, I am willing to overlook the matter, and he can even keep the wood on his land.

By now, at least a dozen cars have pulled up, and their owners have arrived to remonstrate with us for blocking the highway. Discovering the nature of our dispute, however, they immediately forget all about continuing their journeys while there is a confrontation in which to become involved. A committee is quickly sworn in, and the members take it upon themselves to lecture us about the lores and laws of tree ownership. The self-appointed deputation visits the former site of the log pile, and the traffic jam continues to grow. Finally, the committee reaches its decision, which is that they cannot reach a decision. Half of them say that the logs are mine, and half say they are the property of my neighbour. One old farmer says that the tree itself belongs to Mr Moineau Jnr, even though it has stood contentedly on my land for many years.

As more and more passers-by arrive to weigh in with their verdicts, it is clear that we are at an impasse. Then, I am thankful to see help arrive in the shape of a fellow Jolly Boy. The ancient lorry of Marcel Barnard rattles up to join the queue, and our wise friend is quick to calm the situation with a compromise. His proposal is that we take the matter to arbitration in a much more civilised situation and location. Tomorrow, he suggests, we will meet at the Bar Ghislaine to resolve the dispute in the light of day. In the meantime, he will convene a meeting of the village elders, while I will promise to leave the logs on Victor's roof, and Mr Moineau will move his car so that everyone can go about their lawful business.

Grudgingly, my opponent agrees, and after pointedly counting and making a note of the number of logs on Victor's roof, roars off. The roadside committee goes happily on its way to report the details of the dispute to the rest of the region, and Donella, Victor and I continue our slow journey down to the mill cottage. Tomorrow will bring what it brings, but I am no longer the green townie that some of the villagers take me for. As my wife busies herself preparing our evening meal, I spend an hour with Victor, busily swapping the bottom layer of the pile of ash on the roofrack for an identical number of firwood logs.

If the verdict of the court goes against me tomorrow, I shall find some future consolation in toasting my feet in front of the ashwood logs I have managed to salvage. As the countryside poem has it, they will make a fire fit for a king. If my substitution is not spotted, Madame Moineau will also have more than a few words to say to her husband about the holes in her hearthrug which will inevitably result from burning the inferior and volatile pine logs.

Called to the Bar

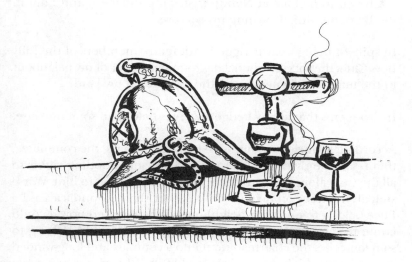

The church clock at Néhou is striking thirteen, and I am in the Bar Ghislaine drowning my sorrows.

In spite of being heavily rigged with fellow members of the Jolly Boys Club, the special tribunal has found in favour of my neighbour in the matter of ownership of the log pile on my land.

It also seems that all my hedgerow trees belong to someone else.

According to ancient countryside law (according to the committee, that is), not only does Mr Moineau have sole wooding rights to all the trees along our party line, but they all belong to him. Worse still, all the trees on my side of the other three boundaries at La Puce belong to my other neighbours. When I asked how it could come to pass that trees growing on my land could belong to someone else, the chairman went into a complex and long-winded explanation which would defy credibility if I had not had some experience in French rural customs, especially when applied to foreigners. Basically, what it boils down to is that everyone in the countryside allegedly owns one meter of their neighbour's land, and my misfortune appears to be that all the trees are on my side of our boundaries; if they were on the other side of the hedge, they would be mine. It is as simple as that. As our chairman says during his summing up, not only was Mr Moineau the Younger not trespassing on my land by stacking his logs on my side of the hedge, it was *I* who had been committing a heinous act by crossing the invisible line marking my land from his. Even more seriously, there was the matter of me attempting to deprive my neighbour of his rightful possessions. Without question, Mr Moineau is the aggrieved party, and his logs must be returned. As I half-expect the chairman to don a black cap, the sentence is passed. Being a reasonable man, my neighbour will accept my plea of ignorance of The Law, and will not press charges. He will be content with my apology and the return of the logs, though the chairman adds pointedly that a small token of my true contrition and remorse in the form of a bottle of scotch or two might not go amiss.

Although feeling betrayed by my JBC colleagues and publicly humiliated in my local bar, I accept the ruling with the best grace I can muster, then go outside to ceremonially hand the disputed logs over. Thinking quickly, I reject Mr Moineau's offer of assistance and tell him I will shift the pile from my car to his as a further demonstration of my remorse. Now completely mollified, he joins the Jolly Boys Club for some mutual backslapping and a re-run of the whole drama, while I start work. The job is made more complex by my having to unload the huge pile of logs from Victor's roof rack and put them on the road before re-loading them on to the roof of the Moineau car, but it is a necessary chore. The inferior pine logs I swapped for the ashwood were at the bottom of the pile on Victor's roof, and must be loaded first on to Mr Moineau's Peugot if he is not to spot my ruse immediately he emerges from the bar. By the time he has uncovered my deception, there will be no witnesses and it will be my word against his. It is a small victory, but better than none. We Brits may not know much about Revolutionary countryside law, but it is not for nothing that we have earned the title of Perfidious Albion.

Finishing the job and ensuring that the ropes securing the load are dangerously but not obviously slack, I return to the bar to smile at my neighbour and scowl at my fellow JBC members. Apart from my subterfuge with the log substitution, my mood has also been improved by hearing the springs of Mr Moineau's Peugeot groan ominously towards the end of the loading process. I do not think that any small French car is man enough to bear the sort of loads that Victor the Volvo finds nothing more than a trifling inconvenience.

*   *   *   *   *

By mid-afternoon, my spirits are fully restored. After mending our broken fences over a few drinks, Mr Moineau and I are getting along almost famously. I have promised to present him with a freshly-shot haggis as well as a bottle of scotch after my next visit to Scotland, while he has promised to give me regular lessons on country etiquette and land management. Knowing that he is a pen-pusher in an office in St Sauveur and having seen the state of the land on the other side of my hedge, I do not think he has much to teach me, but have thanked him for his generous offer. Elsewhere, the regulars are settling down for a relaxing afternoon. By the fire, our resident celebrity chef JayPay is enthralling his audience with a blow-by-blow account of a recent experiment with some fine herbs, dandelion leaves and broiled badger loin. At the bar, René Ribet has been unwise enough to take on the giant Mr Janne in a friendly arm-wrestling match, and Marcel Barnard is happily playing with the Rubik's Cube he bought during Dodgy Didier's last visit. All the squares are the same colour, so he has solved the puzzle at least twenty times in the past hour. Hearing a crash, I turn away from my conversation with Old Pierrot to see that our host Bernard has measured his length on the bar floor. This is not unusual, as Madame Ghislaine's husband always knows when he has had enough, and marks the achievement of this state of grace by simply falling down and resting till he is ready to start again. What is unusual about the incident is that Bernard has performed his party piece on home ground, and while his wife is on the premises. Within seconds, Ghislaine has appeared through the doorway separating the bar area from the grocery department, and we scatter like field mice when the combine harvester hoves into view. Madame Ghislaine, as we have all learned to our cost, disapproves of men in general, and men drinking in particular. Expecting to see her either step over the recumbant figure of her husband to get at us or deliver a swift kick at his body while she has the opportunity, I am amazed to see her rush into her back room and telephone the fire brigade. I know, of course, that the local *pompiers* squad doubles as paramedical emergency cover, but had forgotten that she has never seen Bernard make his celebrated dive for the floor. Madame Ghislaine obviously believes that her husband is ill, not merely legless.

*   *   *   *   *

Given that the traditional three-hour lunch break is barely over, the fire brigade makes good time and less than forty minutes passes before the giant tender screeches to a stop outside the Bar Ghislaine with lights flashing and siren screaming. Although the crew know they are attending a medical emergency rather than a fire, they are obviously determined not to miss out on the dramatic possibilities of the situation, and are dressed and ready for anything. All are in full regalia of helmets and oilskins, and some are actually wearing oxygen tanks and face masks. One is waving an axe as he leaps down from the tender, and seems disappointed to find the door to the bar open wide. The entire population of the village has naturally turned out to enjoy the spectacle, and there are even some small children waving American and British flags left over from the 50th D-Day celebrations. Dogs bark, geese honk, and crows flutter irritably from the church tower as the village cheers the highly-trained squad into action. Unfortunately, the man with the axe of office leads them through the wrong door, and he and his team are soon packed shoulder-to-shoulder in the grocery shop alongside the Bar Ghislaine.

After apologising to the customers for the inconvenience, they leave in an orderly and even subdued fashion, then psyche themselves up again for the assault on the bar. They are to be bitterly disappointed as they arrive in a melee of shouting and shoving to find that Bernard has got his second wind, and is

97

standing by the bar quietly enjoying a glass of the house red.

Protracted negotiations take place, and our host is finally persuaded to resume his position on the floor so that the paramedics can get at him and show their paces. Apparently, they have a wondrous new piece of electronic equipment, and it will be a shame not to try it out in a real-life situation. Within minutes, Bernard is recumbent, still carefully holding his glass of wine as he is hooked up to the machine. As the specially-trained officers of the medical unit study the dials and blinking lights intently, their colleagues remove their facemasks and helmets and take the opportunity for a smoke and drink. To nobody's surprise, Bernard is eventually declared alive, but the paramedic team are loath to miss out on the opportunity for continued drama. There may be complications or some delayed reaction, they argue, so it is necessary for their patient to be rushed to hospital for a more comprehensive check-up. This cheers everyone up except Bernard, but having seen the look on his wife's face, he obviously realises that the hospital at St Sauveur will probably offer a safer refuge than the back room at the Bar Ghislaine. Grudgingly, he agrees to play along provided he is allowed to take his drink and cigarettes with him, and the paramedics spring into action once more. A special collapsible stretcher of the type used for mountain rescues is brought into the bar, and Bernard is strapped safely in. Still carefully balancing the glass of wine, he is carried triumphantly aloft from the bar. Flags wave, the spectators cheer, and the heroes of the hour smile modestly as they clamber aboard the tender, their jobs well done.

A serious bout of handshaking then takes place as their leader apologises to Madame Ghislaine for the delay in attending the emergency. He explains that the problem was caused by a blockage on the road to the village as some fool had made a rotten job of loading logs on his car. He was obviously a townie, the fire chief said scathingly, as half the load was made up of worthless pine faggots.

*   *   *   *   *

The excitement over, I decide to make the weekly visit to my friend the former mayor of Néhou. He will want to know about the drama which has unfolded just across the road from where he sleeps in the village churchyard.

Walking through the rows of immaculately tended graves, I reflect again on the difference between our two cultures when it comes to the final journey we must all take. In France, only three percent of funerals end with a cremation. In Britain, the ratio is reversed. To my knowledge, there is no crematorium in the whole of Cotentin, and my friends could not imagine disposing of a loved one in such a callous way. At the end of November it will be *Toussaint,* and the following day is known as The Fete of the Dead. Then, the little churchyard will be busier than the local supermarket as people gather to decorate their family plots with huge bouquets of chrysanthemums. There will be no forced solemnity or ceremony as children play hide-and-seek around the marble stones; already, they understand the natural cycle of nature which is all around them every day in the farms and countryside, and they know that life and death are indivisible. Now it is their turn to live and grow and make what they can of their lives while they may. Even in Cotentin, people may no longer believe without question in the life eternal, but unlike our more advanced society they do not try to deny that death will always have its day. Although I am learning to appreciate the value of many French rural attitudes, I still find it hard to accept that there is a meaning to it all. For almost half a century Jean and his wife worked their farm and made preparations for their retirement. For five years, I had the privilege of knowing them and learned much about tending the land, and much more about the value of companionship and love. Then, just as they prepared for retirement and a long and peaceful ending to their lifetime together, a car crash left Solange unharmed and her husband dead. As René said at the funeral, it is hard to understand why it could happen to our mayor when there are so many other people we could have done without.

I reach the Chevalier plot, and see that Solange has already made her daily visit. A single flower lies beneath Jean's photograph, and tomorrow it will be changed. Once, I arrived to find her kneeling at the graveside, and did not have the courage to join her. After the tragedy, my wife and I made plans to see her regularly, but we feel somehow guilty at still having each other when she has lost the one she loved so deeply. It is also hard to pass much time with Solange, as she has retreated into a grief so deep that even speaking to her seems an intrusion.

*   *   *   *   *

Not wanting to return to La Puce on the road where Jean and Solange met with the careering lorry, I decide to take the scenic route and drive through the Valley of Néhou. It is really more of a wide plain, and is a pleasant spot to visit at any time. Now, the winter rains have transformed it into a place of almost bewitching stillness and beauty. All through the dry months, the patchwork of tiny fields will be busy with cows and tractors; today, a vast and shimmering lake stretches as far as the eye can see, and the dying winter sun has turned the water to liquid gold.

I park the car, and walk towards the old stone bridge as a heron flaps lazily away from his lunch. It is obviously not Hector, as the bird is quite slim and has no trouble in lifting off from beneath the ancient stone arches. I find a comfortable seat, roll a cigarette and prepare to watch the sun go down. This strange and magical vale is a good place to be on a day like today.

Suddenly, the tranquillity of the scene is shattered, and a wheeling, screaming wing of seagulls scatters in panic as the dull thud of a shotgun echoes across the valley. Somewhere out there in the misty reaches, Death has presented his calling card.

My mood of reverie rudely broken, I decide to see how Mick the Miller is progressing with his labours and coping with the current rainy spell.

Drawing up on the road overlooking the picturesque water mill, I see that there is more water than mill on show at the moment, and I am glad that our little flea is not of the same design. At La Puce, the reservoir system was used because our stretch of the river Lude is in truth no more than a stream, or as one unkind visitor called it last summer, a wet ditch. When the miller at La Puce wanted to go about his business, he would crank down a stone slab at the cascade and divert the Lude into the water meadow, then simply leave the three-acre field to fill up like a giant's bath. When *le reservoir* was full to the brim with millions of tons of water, he would then raise another slab in the corner of the field which overlooks the mill cottage. Obeying the laws of gravity, the water would gush down upon the wheel, filling the buckets attached to the blades and causing it to turn. At the bottom of the cycle, the buckets would empty into the mill pond, and the process would continue until the stone slab was replaced and the flow of water stopped. This simple but ingenious way of harnessing the latent power of even the smallest stream is known as the overshot method, and was used to power the majority of water mills from at least mediaeval times. I have to admit to a twinge of jealously when I first saw the mill at Néhou with its proper river rushing past and the giant mill wheel cranking slowly round. Now I can see that size isn't everything, and can be a considerable disadvantage in a wet Cotentin winter. The raging torrent which the Douve has become boils in frustrated fury as it rushes past the mill, and the rows of sandbags lining the bank will have their work cut out if the river continues to rise.

I walk down the path from the road, and find the inside of the mill has become a swimming pool. The owner is knee-deep in muddy water, and pursuing a floating wardrobe like a shipwrecked mariner desperately swimming after a life raft. As I help round up the flotilla of furniture and move it to higher ground, Michael explains that the river found a way into the mill through the back door on the previous evening, and he has spent the night trying to stem the flood. It has not helped his mood that the radio on

101

the table presently sailing towards the shower room has just broadcast a warning of more rain to come. We wade through to the kitchen, and our friend apologises for not being able to offer me a cup of tea. Without a trace of irony, he tells me that the plumber has not turned up today, so there is no running water on tap. We retreat to the raised ground alongside the mill, and he shows me the illustrations of how the place will look when he has finished the massive programme of works to convert the building into two luxury holiday homes. Come the summer, my friend says bravely, the mill will look like a picture postcard. At the moment, he has made a resolution never, ever again to buy a property which stands so near to water.

I console him by pointing out that it would have been hard to find a water mill any distance from water, and that the odd problem is part of the fun in restoring unusual property in France. I also tell him about the adventures of a couple of our readers who have written to me this morning. They are new settlers, and are restoring a farmhouse further down the peninsula at St Lô. With an unwanted wooden outbuilding to dispose of and having consulted their local equivalent of René Ribet, they had been persuaded to adopt local custom and simply set fire to it. All had gone according to plan until the fire reached a cache of wartime ammunition that had lain buried in the barn for more than fifty years. Apart from the bullet holes in their new septic tank, they report that there was no lasting damage during the barrage, and they have become local celebrities. Along with the fire brigade and television crew, the display of starburst tracer shells had attracted spectators from all around the area, and the mayor has invited them to make a personal appearance and launch the first rocket of the annual firework display on Bastille Day.

On the Road

Spring has returned to La Puce, and with it the first of the year's non-paying guests.

As I opened a downstairs window at the mill cottage this morning, a small bird brushed me aside and flew in with an air that could only be described as proprietary. It circled the room a couple of times, paused to make a special inspection of the kitchen area, then apparently satisfied, left the way it had arrived.

While deeply disappointed that she had not been present to welcome our first yearly regular, Donella was delighted to hear that the tiny wren has booked in for another season. She tells me that it is very unusual for a bird to return to the same nesting site year-on-year, and is sure the creature somehow knows that she and her future family will be comfortable and safe with us.

I agree, but do not see anything unusual or surprising in a visitor deciding to return to a bed and breakfast establishment where not only is the food and accommodation of five star quality, but is also absolutely free. I resign myself to losing the rind off my bacon and the cream from my cornflakes each morning for the foreseeable future. The only consolation is that I will be able to take a lengthy break from the expensive restoration works on the ruined end of the mill. Our guest, as my wife points out, favours a certain niche in the south-facing gable wall, and must not be disturbed by a gang of rough workmen clattering about in their heavy boots.

Having been relieved of my immediate building responsibilities, I suggest that this would be a perfect time for our long-awaited visit to Brittany, where we shall continue the search for Donella's ancestors. Surprisingly, given the appearance of our new lodger, my wife agrees. She is keen to see how far we can go along the branches of her family tree, and I am just as interested. Not being able to trace my paternal forebears back further than three generations, I am enjoying our search for my wife's ancestors.

Our interest began when a distant relative got in touch to say that she had discovered that the family roots lay in Breton, not Welsh, soil. So far, we have been able to establish that Donella's mother's great-great-grandfather was born in Guingamp, and was the illegitimate son of a butcher. Now we will visit the town to see what else we can dig up, and we shall have some valuable assistance. Skimming through a magazine last year, I saw an article by the Scots wife of the pastor of Guingamp, and have enlisted her aid. When we spoke on the telephone, Donella's family connection between Wales and Brittany became even more interesting. The pastor's wife said that many Bretons fled to Wales to escape religious intolerance at the end of the 18th century, and there may well be some interesting archives in the Guingamp library. While I do not see how anyone would choose to go to Wales to escape intolerance, I agree that this is a good lead. We have been promising ourselves a visit to Brittany for some time, and this seems the ideal opportunity. I will not, however, tell our friends at Néhou about the trip and the reason for it. Though they have come to accept us in spite of our being English, learning that Donella has her roots in a foreign country like Brittany could well be too much of a hurdle for the most open-minded Norman to overcome.

I set about preparing for the trip, but am still puzzled by my wife's willingness to leave our visitor to fend for herself. The mystery is solved when I hear Donella on the telephone to Madame Ghislaine. She is not only putting in a large order for cream, bacon and cheese, but is also arranging to have the provisions specially prepared and delivered on a daily basis by Ghislaine's son to the guest wing in the ruined end of the mill. Thus, my wife has broken new ground by extending the facilities at our animal B&B to full room service.

*   *   *   *   *

Before leaving on our journey of discovery, we make a tour of inspection of the grounds and I have a bracing encounter with an intruder. Like an oversized garden gnome, he is sitting comfortably on a tree stump with his line dangling in the foaming waters of the cascade, and has the cheek to bid me a cheery good morning. He also comments that he is having a problem casting his line, and it might be helpful if I were to trim back the branches overhanging his favourite spot. When I recover the power of speech I ask him if he would also like me to fetch him a cup of tea and a piece of cake. My sarcasm is lost on him, and he says no, but a cup of proper French coffee would not go amiss.

After he departs to dry out his clothing, I fish his rod out of the water basin and call our local notaire to ask which methods of killing trespassers are acceptable in this region of France. Predictably, I discover that the laws of the land are not in my favour. Any French fisherman, I am informed, is entitled to cross private terrain to get at a river or stream running through it. Worse still, in the same way that I do not own the trees bordering my land, it seems I do not own the water running through La Puce, or even the fish eating the weed on the river bed. In fact, as the landowner, I (unlike my recent visitor) will have to apply for a permit if I want to enjoy a spot of angling from my river bank. If the person I have just seen off my land had been merely walking across it, I would have been at liberty to maim him in the manner of my choosing. But as he was a true sportsman enjoying his inalienable right to indulge his passion for hunting, I may consider myself lucky if he does not have me arrested.

I thank the notaire for the information, and ask him if it will be alright for me to pick the mushrooms in my woods later this year. He laughs and says of course I may, if I get to them before he does.

*   *   *   *   *

We are well on our way to Brittany, and I have discovered that it is not only in our neck of the woods that drivers are completely mad. Although Victor the Volvo is bowling along at a reasonable rate of knots, his rear bumper seems to exert a magnetic attraction to every French car behind us, and most seem to want to join our luggage in the back. What is particularly galling about this obviously widespread Gallic fetish is that they only do it when the road ahead is perfectly clear. Our tormentors sit for miles on our tail like dogs sniffing a bitch on heat, ignoring all my invitations to pass when there is nothing coming the other way. Even my final gambit of slowing down to a walking pace does not shake them off. Then, just as we reach a blind bend or a juggernaut lorry comes steaming towards us, they overtake with a wave of contempt and a blast on the horn. Dicing with death on the roads is obviously a national sport throughout France, and my fellow motorists are probably spicing up a long journey by playing this dangerous game. After being overtaken by a tractor while we were doing at least 50mph and approaching a narrow hump-bridge already fully occupied by a milk tanker, I lose my nerve and pull off the road for a calming cup of coffee. While at the stop, we phone our daughter Katie in England and gain more evidence of French driving habits and skills at the wheel.

Clearly not wishing to spoil our break in Brittany, Katie tells us the bad news in a roundabout manner. Our car in England has apparently starred on the front page of the local paper. In a recent edition there is a large photograph showing it parked inside a friend's new takeaway shop. The headline writers have had great fun, Katie says, and captioned the picture as showing the first truly drive-in fast food shop in the city. The good news is that our friend Jean-Marie Guedeney is, unlike the car, relatively unmarked by his experience.

One of our closest friends, Jean is a Burgundian who runs a number of highly successful takeaway food shops in Portsmouth. Being French, he refuses to believe that English flour and water can combine to make anything resembling a proper piece of bread, so expensively imports the dough for his filled *baguettes*. Being Burgundian, he also believes that his region produces not only the best bread, cooks, businessmen and lovers in the world, but also the best drivers. Having demonstrated his prowess in all the other areas, he shows off his driving skills by racing around the countryside at weekends and turning every track and lane he visits into a quagmire. During our last visit to England, I could not help but notice that his left leg was encased in plaster to the hip, and innocently asked if he had done the damage while indulging his passion for off-road racing. Outraged, he came up with a rather lame excuse about being kicked by a horse, and said that the most painful result of the accident was his inability to drive his car. His right foot was still able to perform wonders on the accelerator and, on the rare occasions it was needed, the brake, but even a driver of his capabilities found engaging the clutch with his plastered left foot more than an inconvenience. Apart from the taxi fares costing him a fortune as he toured his small empire, he was sorely missing being behind a wheel and in full control of his destination and destiny. As he said this, he looked meaningfully at my old three-litre Granada automatic, and the penny dropped. As I would not be needing it while in Normandy, I replied, he would be welcome to use it till his leg got better. If, I cautioned, he was sure that he could handle such a powerful British car. When he had recovered his composure, my friend reminded me that I of all people should know that the only guaranteed method of enraging a Frenchman was to imply that he was either a bad cook, lover or driver. He would be happy to supply me with a detailed list of several hundred witnesses as to his prowess between the sheets in his pre-marriage days, and would gladly produce a copy of his bank balance to demonstrate his fiscal abilities. As to his driving skills, the cups and medals vying for space on his mantlepiece should be evidence enough. Forbearing to point out that a British sense of humour seemed to be one area in which he was not overly qualified, I handed him the keys and said he would, of course, be welcome to use the Granada till his leg healed, but made him promise to treat the car gently as she was not used to excessive speeds or rough handling.

As I feed coins into the telephone box, Katie comes to the *dénouement* of the story of how our second car has become an overnight celebrity in Portsmouth. Apparently, Jean had driven it to make a final inspection of his latest outlet on the eve of the official opening and check that all was well. The advertisements had been booked, the guests invited, the area circulated with leaflets, and the shop completely refitted. Arriving outside and noting that the expensive display counters were also in place in the shop window, and the signwriter delicately finishing his task, Jean was pleased to find a parking space in the series of bays facing his new premises. Forgetting in his eagerness to buy a parking ticket and being warned of a traffic warden in the offing, he had returned to the car, and noticed that the front tyres were pinched against the gutter. A considerate person, he had taken the trouble to lever himself behind the wheel again so that he could reverse a few inches. According to Jean, his mobile phone rang just as he was about to engage the automatic shift into reverse, and his attention was distracted. Probably due to a fault in my car, he claimed, the engine somehow became stuck in a forward gear. Matters were not helped as his plastered left foot somehow became trapped between the brake and the accelerator, and the car rocketed forward, over the pavement and through the plate glass window. As the signwriter crawled from the wreckage and odd pieces of the shopfront settled on the roof of my car, Jean finally answered the call from his wife, Kathy. Having told her that he was in the new shop, he then had to tell her that he was also still in my car, and the official opening would have to be delayed for a little while. His mood was not helped by the arrival of the press photographer who was attending to discuss the best shots for the opening ceremony the next day. Nor by the somewhat heavy humour of the traffic warden who encouraged him to look on the bright side, as by moving the car off the road he had avoided a stiff parking fine.

Meet the Ancestors

Going strictly on first impressions, Brittany is exactly the same as our part of Normandy, only obviously more affluent and not afraid to show it. A sort of Cotentin with attitude.

Guingamp is like any prosperous market town in our region, but with a number of imposing civic buildings where the budget obviously allowed for embellishment as well as the basics. There is also a particularly impressive gothic cathedral which dominates the centre of the old quarter. Pleasingly, and unlike most old towns anywhere, Guingamp does not appear to suffer from a sprawling suburban area of newer housing. But if the architecture in Brittany seem familiar, the direction signs and public notices do not. A frequent visitor to Wales, I am used to seeing English directions subtitled in Welsh for the exclusive benefit of the 0.05% of natives who need to be told in their own language where the motorway is. Here, it is even more bizarre to see signs in a foreign language with an even foreigner translation beneath. What is particularly puzzling is that, unlike the other European languages which have their roots in Latin, Breton seems to have been made up deliberately to spite and confuse the rest of France. If the language is so patently different from French, however, the inhabitants of Guingamp look remarkably similar to our Norman friends. Everyone we see as we park near the square and take a stroll is very dark and very short. The main difference lies in the relative neatness of their features, and the women are, unlike in our part of Normandy, generally more attractive than the men. Interestingly, most of the males we see seem to be as long in the body as they are short in the leg. I have a regular correspondence with a settler in the Lot who is Welsh and a former head teacher in Newcastle, and he has made a study of this condition. Neville has an interesting turn of mind and a huge intellect, and has formed a theory that evolution and natural selection has resulted in any mining area having more than its fair share of stocky men with long bodies and short legs. He has taken and collated inside leg measurements and other vital data in mining regions in Britain and is now convinced that his theory has, as they say in the academic research business, legs. I am a prime example of the condition which my wife describes as duck's disease and can see his point about this being the ideal shape for working below ground in confined spaces, but I don't know of too many mines in Hampshire, Normandy or Brittany.

Another basic difference between Normans and Bretons seems to be in the character of the people. We have already passed several Guingampians who have actually smiled at us for no good reason, and Donella says she heard the sound of laughter and people generally enjoying themselves in a bar we passed earlier.

Deciding to investigate, we retrace our steps and enter what looks like a typical PMU betting shop and bar. Inside there is the usual throng of punters with faces wrinkled in concentration as they fill in their forecasts for the day's racing, but there the similarity with our home region ends. The décor is lavish in comparison with our local betting shop, and all the chairs and tables appear to have a full complement of legs. At the far end there is an even more incongruous sight. The lady busily taking bets and paying out the winners from her seat at a space-age computer is operating through a window in what appears to be a perfectly-preserved late mediaeval wall, complete with gothic gargoyles and flying buttresses. Right alongside a wonderfully executed arched entranceway is a shiny green door leading to the toilet facilities. After looking at this meeting of the new and old worlds, I ask a customer about the feature. Barely pausing to look up from his calculations, he explains that we are looking at the sole remnants of the ancient town wall. When application was put in to build the betting shop, permission was granted as long as the wall was left unharmed. It was a good way of bringing culture to the people, he says with the air of a man whose logic is indisputable, as many more locals visit the betting shop at Guingamp than would otherwise bother to make a dedicated journey to traipse around a ruin.

As I marvel at this classic example of French pragmatism, Donella orders the coffee and immediately attracts every dog in the bar. She would probably like to think that it is her animal magnetism at work, but I know it is because she has the sugar bowl. It was not till we came to France that I realised just what a sweet tooth most dogs have, and how much they like crunching sugar cubes. In England, of course, granulated sugar is the fashion and dogs are treated like pariahs at virtually all catering establishments. In moments, the bowl is empty and my wife has gone for reinforcements and to ask the various owners if it is alright to feed their pets. As they look at her as if she had asked them if smoking is allowed in the bar, I steal a lump for my coffee from between the teeth of a large German Shepherd, and reflect on the cross-Channel cultural differences in matters of healthy eating. I heard on the BBC recently that sugar has been declared the new dietary public enemy number one, and that some nutritionists are even saying that we should avoid certain fruit and vegetables with a high natural sugar content. On this side of the water, most ordinary people believe simply that a varied diet is the key to good health. As long, that is, as the variation includes regular lashings of sugar, cream, butter, eggs, cheese and at least twenty full-strength cigarettes a day.

*   *   *   *   *

Refreshed by our visit to the PMU, we leave the car and go to meet our guide in the search for my wife's Breton ancestors. Christine Monclair proves to be another interesting addition to our collection of settler friends. From the east coast of Scotland, she has various degrees in history and language, and an obvious and infectious enthusiasm for learning about other cultures, people and their pasts. Soon after arriving at the couple's comfortable apartment, we are taking coffee and enjoying a whirlwind summary of Brittany's long and troubled history from Christine's husband Alain. A true Breton who can trace his own ancestors back for the best part of a thousand years, the Protestant pastor of Guingamp has the typical sturdy build and colouring of his race. He also has what we are to discover is a typical passion for all things Breton, and very little enthusiasm for anything remotely French in origin. Over the next hour, he tells us a story of betrayal, annexation and foreign interference with a zeal and fire which would make the most rabid Welsh National Party activist appear quite moderate. He is speaking in Breton with Christine translating, and I get the feeling that she is, if anything, toning down his views on past French dealings with his region. At the end of a fascinating hour, I thank him and apologise for my lack of command of the French language, which he seems to find more pleasing than offensive. I also persuade Donella to sing a verse from *Land of My Fathers* in Welsh, which puts the seal on our friendship, as he says the language is very similar to Breton, and therefore far superior to any other.

*   *   *   *   *

Later that day, and we find ourselves sitting in the Guingamp library, poring over the town records of births, marriages and deaths for 1751. Despite the entries being in ancient Breton and made in the idiosyncratic hand of a long-dead curé after a hard day at the font, altar and probably communion wine, we have made remarkable progress.

Already, we have traced Donella's ancestors back another three generations, and the Le Cornec family appear to have been substantial and respectable members of the community. Christine

Monclair has had to leave us to carry on the research alone, but has been invaluable in showing us the key words and phrases to look for. *Illegitime* seems to be the word most associated with my wife's ancestors and their activities, but Christine has assured us that this was quite normal for these times. More impressive has been our discovery of not only the name but the address of one Henri Le Cornec, master butcher and husband of a Marie Le Moal. As it will be dusk in an hour and we cannot resist the idea of searching for Donella's ancestral home, we thank the librarian and share a smoke with her before setting off on our pilgrimage. It would be too much to hope that we can find any traces of the original butcher's shop, but hopefully, the *rue montbareil* may still exist.

*   *   *   *   *

Though neither my wife nor I are particularly prone to a belief in the supernatural, we both agree that strange forces seem to have been at work from the moment we arrived in Guingamp. Returning to our car after our session in the library, we go into a nearby *tabac* and ask the owner if he has heard of Montbareil Street. He looks at me rather oddly, then takes me outside and points at the plaque on the wall above his shop. He has not only heard of the street, he says, but he and his family before him have lived and traded in it for many generations. In fact, we are standing in it now. Unfortunately, his local knowledge of other traders does not go back two centuries, but he is sure there are no butchers' shops in the vicinity. Undeterred, we walk along the pleasant street, and stop to take photographs of the monastery and brewery standing in a row of imposing town houses. We are obviously in a wealthy quarter of the old town, and my wife is already beginning to adopt a slightly patronising air when the discussion turns to my own humble roots in Glasgow's notorious Mary Hill district. With the light fading, we make our way to the nearby cathedral, and I pose Donella in front of the giant doors for a final snap. As I look through the viewfinder, the name on the plaque above her head comes into focus. The street is named for Henri Le Moal, who was the chief architect of the restoration of the cathedral in the 16th century. Inside, we find more plaques and tributes to the Le Moals, and acting completely out of character, my wife begins accosting passers-by to tell them of the family connection. At one stage she poses beside a statue of an 18th century Moal and asks if I can see the likeness. With difficulty, I persuade her to leave, and we go off to celebrate the day's work.

Eating In

Before exploring the fleshpots of Guingamp, we decide to buy the makings of a picnic to eat in our hotel. Most of the food shops are still open, and the budget hotel we are staying in boasts neither a restaurant nor room service. I did spot a brochure for a local pizza shop with a delivery service, but we are in the mood for a truer taste of Brittany. Besides, I don't know the Breton for 'Thin crust Napoli Supasize with extra anchovies and can you make sure that there are no stones in the olives, please?'

Having window-shopped the length of the high street, we select an appropriately lavish *patisserie* and enter. As with many places of this nature, the lady behind the counter looks like a beauty consultant on the perfume counter of a department store. Her face is as brightly and artfully decorated as the cakes on display, and her imposing bouffant hairstyle is like a reflection of the spun-sugar confections on the counter between us. She is also wearing the inevitable tailored suit and giant floppy bowtie, and her fingernails look as though they have been dipped in fresh blood. As usual, there is now an embarrassing interlude while my wife tries to decide upon the few cakes and pastries she does not like. While I try to engage the manageress in a conversation about the interesting architectural features of the betting shop along the road, Donella finally makes her agonising choice, which includes some interesting-looking bridge rolls stuffed with all sorts of exotic meats and cheeses. Rather than be pleased that we will have virtually cleared her stock of leftovers, however, the woman gives the all-too-familiar gallic shake of the head, and says that we cannot have the rolls. I ask if they are already booked, but she says no, they are to be thrown away at closing time. I ask if they are past their sell-by date, and when she understands what I am talking about she looks shocked and says certainly not. The fact is that the rolls must be eaten hot and the ovens in the bakery have been turned off for the day. I then ask if there is not a microwave on the premises, and her bouffant appears to swell and crackle at the insult. Trying to placate her, I say that we are only English, and will be quite happy to eat them cold. With a withering look, the woman agrees that, being English, we would probably not mind the insult to their creator, but she would. With that, she takes the rolls from the display case and carefully puts them out of sight under the counter. Not wishing to lose the rest of our supper, I submit, but get my own back by asking if she has any HP brown sauce to give her veal and wild goose *vol-au-vents* a little more flavour.

*   *   *   *   *

We arrive at the hotel, and are greeted by an almost surreal spectacle in the reception area. A number of large lorry drivers and weary commercial travellers are slumped in their chairs looking with complete mystification at a television set on a shelf in the corner. I hear the rapid French dialogue interspersed with canned laughter, and at first think that the viewers are all Breton, and pretending not to understand the foreign language. Then I look up and see that they are numbly watching a dubbed version of the British sitcom *'Allo 'Allo.* As we climb the stairs to our room, we discuss the entertainment value in Brittany of a comedy programme about a café in Occupied France where nearly all the jokes are puns which depend upon the characters apparently mispronouncing French in English.

Eating Out

Our midnight feast at the Guingamp Kwik-Stay is over, and we have voted it the best hotel meal we have had since our visit to the south last year. We actually use hotels rarely, preferring to stay above bars or in *chambre d'hôtes* when we cannot impose ourselves on an English settler in the area. In our experience, food in French hotels is usually overpriced to make up for the low cost of the rooms. There are some notable exceptions, and we cherish them.

Early last year, we were on our way to visit friends in the deep south. As usual, I had underestimated the journey time, and overestimated the availability of accommodation in the depths of winter. Some hours earlier we had passed a seedy bar on the outskirts of what looked like the location for the shooting of *The Village of the Damned*, and my wife had suggested we stop and make the best of it.

In a sulk I refused. As per our marital agreement, I had blamed her poor navigation for the situation, though it had been my idea to go by the scenic route rather than stay on the motorway. Now, dusk was falling, and we were hopelessly lost in a strange and increasingly desolate place. Despite the evidence, I was still in denial, even after my wife pointed out an interesting rock formation which looked ominously similar to one we had passed an hour before. Irritatingly, all the names on the map seemed to end with -ac, but none of them agreed with the road signs we occasionally passed. As it grew darker, it began to snow, the road narrowed, and the signs petered out altogether. The petrol gauge had been hovering on zero for some time, and I was promising Victor the Volvo anything if he would just last out till we arrived at the next service station. Overall, the situation was getting serious. Then, just as my wife said she thought she could hear a wolf howling, we emerged from a pass between two gigantic slabs of rock, and saw civilisation. There on a hilltop was the brooding outline of an ancient bastille town, its grim walls and towers standing out against the silvery night sky. As far as I could see at this range, there were no suspiciously large bats circling the battlements or villagers with flaming torches laying siege to the keep, so in our situation it looked almost welcoming. And it was only a mile away. At least, it was only a mile away as the bat flies. As we crawled upwards in an ever decreasing spiral, the road got narrower, the snow fell with ever increasing intensity, and the precipice alongside the road got steeper.

Then, as Victor was beginning to fight for breath and I was contemplating ending our misery with a quick wrench upon the steering wheel, we reached the end of the corkscrew climb and limped through a giant stone archway and in to the cobbled square, where we found the town to be completely deserted. Although in familiar France, we seemed to be in another, stranger world. Either we had entered a different dimension and time-zone immediately after leaving the motorway, or the entire community were at a goat-sacrificing ceremony in the next town.

After making a crude crucifix from my car jack and lever, I led the way through the empty streets. Eventually, we saw a single light, dimly filtering through the closed shutters of a gaunt stone building. An old van stood outside, and there were steps up to a pair of double doors, and what looked like the outline of a human body on a faded sign above the entrance. Either it was an hotel or the town mortuary. Looking at each other and the desolated streets and snow-filled sky, we silently considered our alternatives and entered.

Inside, we found a huge vaulted room with flagged floor, a cat with three legs, several trestle tables and a selection of customers who looked at us as if they had run out of goats for next week's coven meeting. Crossing the floor to the sound of our own footsteps, we smiled weakly, and I tried not to look for a bolt through the giant barman's neck as I ordered our drinks. As I spoke, the muttered conversation in the room ceased, and the atmosphere became, if possible, even colder. Unable to summon up the nerve to ask about accommodation, I led the way to a corner seat, put my back to the wall and started drawing up an escape plan. We had always sought out unusual places to stay during our trips around France, but this was beyond the pale. Swiftly finishing our drinks, we got up, and staying close together, sidled back to the bar to pay. As I debated waiting for the change or making a break for it while his attention was diverted, I saw the barman frowning at the money I had given him and realised it was a twenty pound note. Holding it up to the light, he looked at it and then me, and asked suspiciously if we were English. Thinking quickly, I explained that I was actually more than half Scottish on my father's side, and my wife's mother came from Wales. In our travels I find this is usually the safest bet in a strange and hostile setting. To my knowledge neither Scotland nor Wales has ever colonised, occupied or been at war with any foreign power except the English. However, the way things were going, this could be the one town in Europe invaded and conquered by an away team from the Cameron Highlanders. For a moment, the giant scratched his head where his left ear should have been while he looked us up and down, then bared his teeth in what could just have been a smile. From then on, the atmosphere was to change dramatically. Our new friend barked a few words at the customers, gave me back my banknote and asked us if we had anywhere to stay for the night. As we relaxed over another drink, he explained that my size and our strange accents had given the impression that we were Germans. Every man in the bar had lost a relative to local attrocities during the war, he went on, and return visits from the *Bosche* were not exactly encouraged. Hearing that

we were lost, he insisted that we stay for the night, and shortly
showed us up to a suprisingly comfortable room. Hungry but at
least having found shelter for the night, we were preparing to go
to bed when a heavy knocking rattled the solid oak door in its
frame. Opening it tentatively, I was confronted with a man who
looked like the barman's bigger and uglier brother. He was dressed
in grimy chef's whites, and more importantly, carrying a large
cleaver. As I began to babble that we had never even visited
Germany, he interrupted me to tetchily enquire if we were coming
down for the gourmet evening. There were only two seats left,
and the *aperitifs* would be served in exactly twelve minutes.

We were downstairs in less than five, and found the bar transformed.
The trestle tables had been dressed with white linen tablecloths,
and the customers and cat had obviously gone to the goat barbecue.
In their place, a throng of smartly dressed diners were sitting in
obvious anticipation of the treat to come. Hurriedly, we found
our places and joined them.

Over the next three hours, we were to be transported to culinary
heaven. I am the first to agree with my wife that I am a *gourmand*
rather than a *gourmet*, but even I could tell that we were in the
presence of an eating experience as unique as our surroundings.
There were a full five courses, each accompanied by a different
wine, and each based upon a central theme of the fruits of the
local streams, fields and forests. There were mushrooms the size
of parasols, and cheek of wild boar with a skin that crackled and
echoed around the hall like gunshot fire. There was hare, trout
and other mysterious animal titbits which I relished, but chose
not to have identified by our ever-attentive waiter. There were
even five different textures and types of local bread, some stuffed
with crisp golden nuggets of walnut. After each course came an
oral examination, conducted by the giant chef, who visited every
table after each course to demand frank comment on his offerings.
He said he would equally accept praise and constructive criticism,
and it was a mark of the quality of the meal that not a single diner

complained or even made a helpful suggestion for future reference. In my experience, this is almost unheard of in France, even with a meal of those standards. I like to think it was because our table could not find a single thought as to how the feast could have been enhanced, but it might have had a little to do with the fact that our *chef de cuisine* was still carrying his cleaver.

Next day, the snow lay deep and crisp and fairly even upon the cobbles of the square as we drove contentedly through the giant archway. Reaching the road at the bottom of the hill and heading back to civilisation, we swore that we would return one day.

If only, that is, we would ever be able to find the place again.

Shopping Around

It is to be our last morning in Brittany, so we decide to stock up on local delicacies. They will make ideal gifts for the settlers we shall be staying with during our journey back to La Puce. It is only a little more than three hours from Guingamp to North Cotentin, but we do not wish to miss the opportunity of testing out our pension plan. Studying the map before leaving La Puce, I see that we have several readers and correspondents in Brittany who have been rash enough to invite us to drop in any time we are passing. I believe that a bottle of reasonable wine and a round of cheese is more than adequate exchange for a night's accommodation, given that our hosts will also have the gift of my company and sparkling conversation. My wife believes they will get the worse side of the deal, and forecasts that, after an initial visit, many of my fans will move home and not tell us. Or in extreme cases, opt for repatriation.

As we are in the region, we also owe a duty call to Les Miserables and his wife Ono. These are not their real names, of course, but should be. Les has been in the depths of despair since making the crossing to settle in Brittany. We have rather cruelly dubbed his unfortunate wife 'Ono' because this is what she says when their latest mishap occurs. As we have found over the past year, she says it very often.

*   *   *   *   *

In a Guingamp supermarket, we buy a selection of regional foodstuffs and line up at the check-out. As I hand over our credit

130

card, we become part of yet another demonstration of attitudinal differences on either side of the Channel. After swallowing my card, the machine on the desk gurgles unhappily for a few moments, then falls silent. Shrugging unconcernedly, the check-out girl pushes it in again and continues her conversation with a friend at the back of the long queue now forming behind us. In England, I would be sweating with embarrassment, and trolley rage would have flared. The people behind us would have been sighing dramatically, looking at their watches, diving off to another desk or even offering to pay our bill if only we will get a move on, and I would already bear the imprint of a trolley front on my buttocks. Here, an exactly opposite mood is fostered as customers crowd around to exploit the opportunity for a bit of problem-solving. Helpful advice comes from all sides on various insertion methods, ranging from turning the card upside down, bending it in half, or just giving the machine a good kicking. An off-duty electrician in the queue even whips out his screwdriver and offers to take the box to pieces. By now, a huge crowd has gathered, and not one of the customers behind us seems in the slightest bit worried about completing their transactions. Rather than looking at me suspiciously and asking pointed questions about our credit balance, the staff are united in being the first to come up with an amicable solution. Finally, as the market place outside drains of shoppers and it becomes difficult to move inside the store, the manageress makes her way towards us with a measured tread. She does not actually pull on rubber gloves as she approaches, but has the quietly confident air of a top neuro-surgeon about to perform a particularly demanding operation for the benefit of a theatre full of trainees.

With a flourish, the manageress takes the card, puts on her glasses and examines it as a respectful hush falls on the gathering. Then she nods knowingly, spits delicately on the metal strip, wipes it on her capacious bosom and returns it to the check-out girl. We all wait breathlessly as the gurgling sound strikes up again, and is followed by a whirring and clattering before my card is given

131

the all-clear. Spontaneous applause breaks out and is graciously accepted with a nod of the head before the manageress returns to her eyrie, and we are slapped on the back and congratulated as if we have just scooped the jackpot on the state lottery.

*   *   *   *   *

The excitement over, we wave goodbye to our audience, spot a specialist grocery store next door and wander in to top up our possessions. Here, we are to see another side of the French attitude to customer service.

As we breathe in the heady aroma of huge rounds of cheese stacked like wheels in a tyre repair centre, the shopkeeper emerges through a beaded curtain and looks us up and down. Apparently, we pass muster. I know this because he enquires as to our needs with a fractional jerk of his head and miniscule movement of the eyebrow which can say or ask a hundred different things in French. He is small and dark with a long body and short legs, so obviously on home territory. I open the proceedings by apologising for speaking French like a Spanish cow, which always breaks the ice in Normandy. Here, it has little effect. The proprietor yawns, scratches his goatee beard and looks out of the window as if to see what interesting activities are occupying other people's lives. Flustered by his lack of response, I say the first thing that comes into my head, and ask if he has any cheese. Now both eyebrows come into play, the beret is removed and the bald head scratched while the shoulders lift a full centimetre to register his incredulity at the question. Our man obviously believes in energy conservation. Rising to the bait, I then employ a little English body language by narrowing my eyes, straightening my shoulders and puffing out my chest in preparation for the battle ahead. It is a pity about my moustache, because I can't also show off my rapidly stiffening upper lip.

Some time later, and we are sharing Victor with more than twenty painstakingly wrapped and tied packages of cheese, each no more than a few grams in weight. The whole process of my careful study, sampling and final purchase took more than an hour, and I made sure that nearly all of our selections came from giant cheeses at the bottom of each pile. With any luck, the sour-faced shopkeeper will have a sore back to remember us by, if not a lot of money in the till.

As we wave goodbye to the town of her ancestors, my wife can delay trying the samples no longer, and fishes around in the box to find the morsel of Morbihan cheese that was my final choice. About to unwrap the package, she stares at the wrapper, then silently holds it up for me to see. I wait till we get rid of a moped which is apparently trying to hang itself on Victor's back bumper like a dinghy on the back of a yacht, then read the name of our cheese specialist. Of all the shops in Guingamp, we have somehow been steered into the premises of one Henri Le Cornec.

My wife is overcome with emotion, and wants us to return to the town so that she can tell Mr Cornec that they must be related, but I persuade her against the idea. Probably, I gently point out, Cornec is the Breton equivalent of Smith or Jones, and the disappointment would spoil our visit for her. Much better to write and ask Christine to pursue any family connection, I suggest. We drive on in silence as I mull over the possibility that my wife and the sulky shopkeer are, in fact, related. Now I think of it, Donella's mother was, for some reason, rather taciturn with me, and also short and dark. I consider asking Donella if any members of her family apart from her great aunt ever sported a beard, but decide against it, and concentrate on my driving.

Rain Gods

Above us the Brittany sky is an untroubled azure, but a single dark cloud lies anchored directly above the valley ahead. Les Miserables and his wife Ono must be at home.

We first heard from the Miserables when they wrote to ask our advice about moving to France. They were fed up with their undeserved misfortunes and betrayals at the hands of so-called friends in England, and planned to sell up and escape to where life was simpler and people more trustworthy. Their idea, they said, was foolproof. They would, quite literally, go back to their ancestors' rural roots. Having sold their apartment on the south coast and invested half of the profit, they would buy a picturesque cottage with a lot of land somewhere deep in the heart of France. They would have a cow for their milk, chickens for their eggs, and grow acres of organic vegetables. The surplus would be sold to or traded with the local baker, butcher and even bank manager. In his spare time, Les would build a holiday cottage or two for summer letting. With the experience gained from her window boxes in Brighton and evening-class sessions in flower arranging, Ono would grow orchids and other exotic blooms for sale at market. The final clincher in their argument was that they had visited France on several occasions, and enjoyed themselves immensely. It would all seem just like being on holiday for ever.

The Miserables planned to make the move as soon as possible, and had had the good fortune to meet a man in a pub who was, he had told them, a top financial consultant. He would secure them the maximum return on their money, and leave them to get on with living the good life. All they needed now was to decide on exactly where in France to settle. As they both suffered from incipient arthritis and would need plenty of sunshine and dry heat for the orchids, they had decided to plump for the deep south, and liked the idea of Brittany. Did we think that Bretons would be keen on organically-grown British onions, and did we not agree that their carefully thought-out plan of action was a sure-fire winner?

My letter in return was as usual more difficult to compose than any book I have written. I had heard all this before, and could usually predict the outcome with pinpoint accuracy. While not wanting for one moment to put them off turning their dream into reality, I finally responded, had they really thought it all through? Their ideas were basically sound, but could perhaps benefit from further examination.

For instance, were they sure that the average rural French bank manager would increase their credit facilities in return for a regular supply of organic vegetables? Would Les's undoubted ability in DIY equip him to build a couple of houses from the ground up? Also, Brittany was not exactly in the deep south of France, and we had found that most of the inhabitants already knew their onions, and were keenest on the home-grown variety.

Predictably, my letter received a chilly reply, and the next we heard was a rather triumphal phone call to inform us that the Miserables had made their move in spite of our reservations, and were now settled happily in a cottage in the heart of the Côtes d'Armor. That is, they would be settled happily as soon as the property was truly theirs. Les explained that they had instantly settled on the first house the local agent had shown them because it was a snip (or at least, the agent had said it was a snip), and at least four other English buyers were in a race to buy it. There was also a considerable amount of land surrounding the property, and the house had been scrupulously restored by the owners.

The rusty corrugated iron roof, their agent had pointed out, was actually a strong selling feature, as this was one of the few remaining examples of traditional Breton craftsmanship in the area. Anxious not to miss the moment, the Miserables had signed all the necessary papers, sold their apartment in England at a cut price for the sake of expediency, and moved over to their dream home in France. Les added that they had been particularly impressed with the way their agent had casually given them the keys and invited them to move in with all their furniture even before the final contracts had been exchanged. It was all so French, informal and trusting.

The next call came less than a week later. According to the Miserables' agent, a long-lost daughter of the vendors had appeared, and was proving reluctant to agree to the sale. Thoughtfully, the owners were not insisting that the Miserables move out of their future home, but of course they would now have to pay a fair rent until the matter could be resolved.

From then on we received at least one call a month, each bringing more bad news from Brittany. His voice descending into ever-deepening gloom as he detailed the latest disaster, Les would report on a catalogue of woes that finally convinced us that the Miserables were, in fact, not merely exceptionally unlucky. They were rain gods. As we of all people knew, nobody could expect a completely trouble-free passage when moving to a foreign country and culture and changing one's lifestyle completely. But whereas a little rain must be expected to fall into every life, the Miserables seemed to be spending theirs in a permanent downpour.

*   *   *   *   *

Approaching the Miserables' house, I switch the lights and wipers on as we enter the rain zone starting at their front gate. My wife remarks rather unkindly that at least they are assured of plenty of water for the vegetable plot.

138

We park Victor next to a car with a broken axle and run to the front door, which I notice has been hung upside down. Looking at the bare wires behind the bell-push, I settle for knocking, and take care not to dislodge the one hinge which is holding the door roughly in place. Eventually, Ono appears, and is obviously trying to be brave. She welcomes us in with a caution to avoid the brimming bucket in the passageway and the holes in the floor. Shouting above the relentless drumming of the rain beating down on the tin roof, I comment on the weather and she says that it is not as bad as when they arrived. Donella then makes the mistake of observing that their cat Claude must be enjoying his new-found freedom, and there is a painful scene as Ono breaks down while telling us that he has gone missing, and it is said he has been shot by local hunters. It is not that they would have mistaken him for a legitimate wildlife target, she says. Cats are routinely despatched on sight for having the temerity to kill baby rabbits before they grow large enough for shooting by the human hunters.

Awkwardly, we enter the living room and are greeted by our host, who apologises for not being able to shake hands properly due to the bandages. As we take coffee, he explains that their plans for building the rustic holiday cottages in the garden have had to be put on hold. Not because of his accident with the electric saw, he assures us, but because they have nowhere to build them. The field alongside the cottage that they thought was theirs was apparently not included on the sale agreement, and the owners want a premium price for it because of the rich and fertile soil it offers. Ono sniffs and says it must be more fertile than the plot in front of their house, where the earth only goes down for two inches, after which it is solid rock. This discovery has put paid to their vegetable-growing plans.

After an embarrassing silence while we refrain from posing any further questions for fear of what the answer might be, my wife asks where their toilet is. Les responds rather bitterly that she will find it in a showroom in St Malo, with the rest of the bathroom they have had to order. He goes on to explain that when the previous owners told them that they were taking the bathroom fittings with them, he had thought that they were referring to the towel rails and medicine cabinet. The Miserables had arrived back from the notaire's office on the day of the exchange and found an empty room with pipes sticking up from the floor. They had also found that the pipe from the former toilet pan led no further than the outside wall of the cottage, where what they had assumed to be a septic tank has turned out to be merely a shallow hole in the ground. The problem of fitting a proper disposal system will be compounded because of the solid rock just beneath the surface.

Later, Les takes me on a tour of the house, and when I ask about the prospects for providing bed and breakfast facilities, he says that they will first need some bedrooms to put the beds in. They had not visited the upstairs of the house when the agent showed them round, or they would have realised that it is nothing but a windowless loft. He had not then understood the French tradition of using spare rooms on the ground floor as bedrooms, and the owners counting the living room, coal hole and even a corrugated iron lean-to in the tally had given a completely misleading impression.

*   *   *   *   *

Later that afternoon, we make our excuses and leave. We cannot bear to hear of any more catastrophes, and besides, Donella does not want to force the Miserables into the coal shed for the night so that we can have their bedroom. Nor does she like the idea of using the chemical toilet which Les has fitted in the kitchen.

As we leave, we promise to keep in touch, wish the Miserables better luck for the future, and Donella presents Ono with a colourful pot of myrtles we had bought in a market earlier that day. Ono examines the flowers, then shakes her head sadly. The tiny scarlet blooms, she says, are not real flowers. They are pieces of material, cunningly wired on to the stems to give the appearance that the plant is in bloom. It is not uncommon practice in this part of France, she says.

Unfortunately, we have been gullible, and been conned into paying out for something that is not what it seems.

We nod sombrely, then beat a hasty retreat up the muddy track and out of the permanent rain cloud, making a pact not to return. As my wife says, while sympathising deeply with their misfortunes, the myrtle incident must make one wonder whether such a degree of bad luck can be catching.

*   *   *   *   *

By the time we reach our alternative accommodation for the evening, we are in a far better mood. Our host is the last person to be taken advantage of, and will surely restore our faith in human fortitude and triumph against adversity.

Madge has been writing to us since she picked up a copy of my first book during a ferry crossing, and wrote to say that Donella seems to be her sort of person. Since retiring, she has kept up a regular correspondence, and has been settled in her converted barn near Avranches for several years. As we arrive, we see that she is well on the way to accomplishing her aim of converting the converted barn back to its original function.

A woman after my wife's heart, Madge thinks a lot more of animals than humans, and her home now shelters many more species than it ever did when it was a barn. She has adopted every stray domestic creature in the area, and even the local wildlife have forgotten their normal differences to take advantage of her hospitality. As we toot the horn to announce our arrival, we set off a cacophony of hooting, honking, barking and braying, and

141

I am sure I recognise some of the birds which petulantly flutter away as we pull to a halt. Perhaps I have solved the mystery of where our wildlife guests go to in the winter. Rather than make the long journey to North Africa until the springtime, they probably stay at Madge's beastly B & B.

A former postmistress in a North Wales hamlet, our elderly friend is naturally coded in our files as Madge The Post. As we are to discover, the locals now know her as the Mad Hornet Woman.

After casually brushing two cats, a hamster, a great dane and a barn owl with a missing ear from the sofa, our hostess invites us to take our ease and join her in a glass of home-made dandelion and burdock and a roll-up made from homegrown tobacco. As we build up a comfortable fug in front of the cheery blaze from the wood-burning stove, Madge cheerfully explains how she came to earn her local sobriquet. When she first bought the ruined barn, she would travel across each month to oversee the construction work and get to know the local wildlife community. After a year, all was finally ready for her to move in, and she arrived with her removal van to find two fire engines and a police car in the yard. The new front door was hanging from its hinges, and several firemen were slumped around the entrance, being given urgent medical treatment by their colleagues. Establishing that she was the new owner, the local chief of police saluted smartly, welcomed her to Brittany, and said that she could now rest easily in her bed, thanks to the self-sacrifice and skill of the local *pompiers*. He went on to explain that a neighbour having seen a great multitude of hornets entering and leaving her premises, the fire brigade had as usual been called in to deal with the menace. In her absence, they had broken in, and discovered what would undoubtedly go down as the biggest nest of *frelon* in the whole of Brittany, if not the whole of France. It reached, he said, from the floor of the attic to the very roof. It was a veritable castle of a nest. With hardly a thought to their own safety, the brave *pompiers* had dealt with the problem, the castle had been breached and the hornets banished. The policeman had, Madge recalled, been totally bemused by her reaction, and by the news that she had not only known about the nest, but had been actively encouraging the hornets to set up home in her attic for more than a year. The police chief was even more astounded to learn that she was now intent on suing the commune not only for the cost of a new door, but for the hurt and mental anguish they had caused her and her lodgers.

*   *   *   *   *

After a fairly comfortable night in company with the regular occupants of the spare bedroom, we thank the Hornet Woman for her hospitality and set out on the final leg of our journey to La Puce. Finding my attention wandering as I try to keep Victor on a fairly straight course, I confide to my wife that I had experienced some very strange dreams during the previous night. Donella then tells me that she too had had a very peculiar dream, involving in her case a talking giraffe, a washing machine and a jar of salad cream. Perhaps, she says, it was the sheep's milk vindaloo we had for supper, or even the dandelion and burdock wine.

I am non-commital, but would rather believe it was Madge's home grown tobacco. The tall growths we saw in the greenhouse looked nothing like any plants I have seen before, excepting during a news story about a drugs squad raid on an illegal cannabis production plant in North Wales.

Educating Rita

Back on home territory, we are on the last leg of our journey from Brittany, and will pop into our favourite English local in France.

We turn off the coastal road and head for The Lobster Pot pub and restaurant, and I narrowly avoid a flock of crows squabbling over a grisly collection of skin and fur in the road. On reflection, the crows are more likely to be rooks. There is a saying in Cotentin that if you see a flock of crows they are probably rooks, and if you see a solitary rook it is probably a crow. It is a mark of my level of acclimatisation to the way people think in this region that I can follow the logic of this argument with no difficulty. I'm told that there are other more subtle ways of telling the difference between the two species, but have never been close enough to a live or dead crow or rook to make an intimate examination. Fellow members of the Jolly Boys Club also say that the cawing of rooks and crows is entirely different, and that Old Pierrot can tell the differences between the individual birds which frequent his land, has given them all names, and can even speak their language. However, from what I have heard, this familiarity doesn't seem to stop him shooting them at every opportunity. So far, I have not tried out his recipe for rook pie, which he says was a local delicacy hundreds of years ago. According to the oldest member of our community, and most certainly the oldest person in all France if his claims are remotely true, the dish was somewhat like a flan, decorated with wing feathers and the complete head of the bird as the centerpiece. It has, says old Pierrot, been a particular favourite of his since he first tried it on the original Bastille Day.

I am sure my leg is being pulled, but it is true to say that we have heard of little that has once lived and moved that our neighbours and friends will not eat in some guise or other. The other day, I saw a woman buying what appeared to be a blackcurrant jelly from the mobile butcher's van on its weekly visit to Néhou. I asked what it was, and he said it was a specially delivered treat for the birthday party of the woman's youngest child. He went on to explain that it was not jelly, but half-congealed pig's blood, which must be rushed directly from the throat cutting ceremony to the oven and cooked to the exact glutinous consistency to retain all its flavour. Most real countrypeople prefer to eat the delicacy straight from the oven, he explained, and some even straight from the pig itself. Hopefully, wobbly pig's blood will not be on the bar menu at our favourite English pub today.

*   *   *   *   *

It has been a long drive from the Hornet Woman's home at Avranches, and I am delighted to turn the final bend and see that Mike and Rita are open for business. They have been running The Lobster Pot for more than a year now, and have obviously survived their baptism of fire. In fact, they have done much, much better than anyone who knows anything about running a small business in France would have predicted.

I know from observation and my correspondence that owning a bar and restaurant in France is one of the most popular fantasies for the sort of Britons who like entertaining at home and think that doing it professionally would be just as pleasurable, and profitable to boot. Luckily for them, the vast majority never get to learn the vast difference between cooking for friends for fun and customers for cash. For those who go on to turn their dream into reality, it almost always proves to be a fatal attraction. It is hard enough running a pub or restaurant in Britain, and the catering industry comes above even the building trade in the small business bankruptcy lists each year. Add the difficulties of trying to succeed in the countryside and in a country where they think that foreigners and especially Britons have a problem boiling an egg, and you have a recipe for disaster. Even the French find it difficult to make a rural bar or restaurant pay, and The Lobster Pot is not only isolated, it is in a coastal area where summers are short and winters very long.

When our mutual friend Madame Lynn told us that Mike and Rita were taking over a defunct premises near the west coast and planning to combine an English pub with a French restaurant, we thought they had gone completely mad. To our knowledge, neither had even cooked as much as a pop-tart for profit, and neither could speak more than a few words of French. In bookmaking terms, the odds on their coming through the first year intact would make a bet on Elvis Presley being found alive and well and running a chip shop in Doncaster look attractive.

However, our gloomy forecasts had obviously not allowed for the couple's combined qualities of enthusiasm, imagination, and that most useful of attributes for anyone wishing to make a go of a business in France, sheer bloody-mindedness. As we are to learn, they also have that other vital characteristic for all would-be settlers, the ability to adapt to circumstances and situations. The layout of The Lobster Pot is a perfect example of their flair for combining the best of both worlds and appealing to all sorts of potential customers. The small and cosy bar gives more than a flavour of an English pub, with wrought iron tables, suitably nautical knick-knacks on the wall, and there is even a carpet on the floor. This inspired if sometimes impractical touch is unknown in Cotentin bars, and is a novelty which has attracted sightseers from miles around. Most importantly, the couple have ensured that they have not created a gimmicky Brit-theme pub which would appeal only to homesick expatriots. As Rita says, it was most important that they did not create an English ghetto, full of whingeing settlers who would really much rather be back home. The pub is for the locals and visitors, and virtually everyone is welcome, even people like us.

Another inspired decision by our hosts was to leave all traces of Englishness at the door to the restaurant. Within, the style is of a typically unpretentious French eating house, and the menu and kitchen are entirely in the hands of a local chef. Mike happily admits to being barred from his own kitchen, and will be even happier if this remains the status quo.

Over the past year, the couple had also learned the importance of providing their regulars with more than the range of services an English pub would expect to offer. As we enter, we see a patient farmer sitting with a glass of wine in one hand and a large new bandage on the other. Nurse Rita has obviously been at work. After greetings are exchanged, I guiltily settle my bar bill from the last visit, drinks are ordered and we settle down to catch up on their progress. Rita explains that a vital part of the adaptation process was to educate herself in the various roles and skills necessary for the running of a small pub in the countryside of Normandy. As well as becoming the landlady of the local bar, she has learned to be an effective and obliging counsellor, fortune teller, dispute arbitrator, bank manager and even a bookie's runner and surrogate physician. Apart from treating minor ailments, she also places bets and picks up prescriptions on her regular runs to town, and is obviously enjoying her voluntary service overseas. She makes light of her and Mike's additional services to the community, but it is clear from the attitude of the customers that she and her husband have won the hearts of the locals in a very short time.

But, as they tell us, getting through the year successfully has been a two-way educational process, with some interesting breakdowns in communication occuring on both sides of the bar counter.

These early hiccups included several of the locals confusing a designer pedal-bin in the refurbished toilets for a new-fangled

149

urinal, and the chef asking Rita if she would like a little nookie when discussing a forthcoming Italian theme night. He was, she discovered later and with some relief, merely seeking her opinion on the wisdom of including *gnocchi* pasta dumplings on the menu.

But as Mike told us, more than a few mistakes had also been made on their side of the linguistic fence. On a special fruits of the sea evening, the chef had been close to tears when not a single diner ordered his signature dish of *filet de dorade*, or sea bream. Investigation beyond the kitchen doors eventually revealed that Mike had been practicing his French in the bar by boasting of the chef's choice, but pronouncing the dish not *dorade* as in fish, but *de rah* as in rat.

On another occasion, a French holidaymaker had come into the bar and announced he was on a special tour, tracing the footsteps of *Guillaume le Conquérant* in the area. As the village licensee, did Mike have any special knowledge in the matter of where the great William had been seen locally? Mike apologised and said he had not heard of anyone of that name in the area, but advised his visitor to try the village grocery shop. They if anyone would be sure to know Mr Conquerant's home address.

After the Fox

I t is good to be home again.

We have been on a book-signing tour around Britain, and Donella is in a very bad mood. As usual, our disagreement has started over something trivial, in this case my innocent question as to why women always slam car doors. Within minutes we had moved on to the issue of Why Men Never Put The Toilet Seat Cover Down After Use, and I have not helped matters by pointing out that it would surely be much worse if we didn't bother to lift them *before* use.

No doubt exhausted by having to spend two weeks in cities and away from her beloved La Puce and in the company of humans rather than animals, Donella has made me an offer which she hopes I will not refuse. In future, she says, I can go over and enjoy the limelight on our promotional tours, while she will stay at La Puce and look after the more important responsibilities of keeping the land in trim and feeding her flock. She has also come up with what seems to her to be an ideal compromise. I will continue to make our fund-raising trips to England, and send over the proceeds. With the cheques I may include my dirty washing, and she will launder it and post it back. That way, she says, we will both be getting what we want out of life, and having our basic necessities attended to.

Now that we are back home, I hope her mood will change, and a fortuitous incident soon does the trick. As we are unloading Victor the Volvo, I hear what sounds exactly like the time signal pips on Radio 4, and prepare myself for a tongue-lashing for having left the electricity on in our absence. My wife, however, is transformed with joy, and tells me that any fool should know that what we are hearing is actually a toad. Unimaginative naturalists, she says, would dismiss the sound as a mating call, but she knows that he is welcoming her back home.

To maintain her sunny mood, I agree and try to appear overjoyed at the news. At the same time, I make a mental note to carefully check the contents of my slippers tomorrow morning.

*   *   *   *   *

On the matter of meeting the public and press, I do have some sympathy for my wife, because I know that, apart from missing La Puce, she hates our occasional round-Britain tours as much as I enjoy them. The highlight of this trip has been the major French Property exhibition of the year, and I relished virtually every moment of it. Staged at a hotel in London, the exhibition attracts tens of thousands of visitors, and I take a delight in meeting as many of them as possible during the weekend. Apart from the opportunity of selling books, I also get to hear stories from those in the various stages of realising their dream to own a home in France. The event is also a suitably impressive occasion at which to meet the nation's travel writers and book critics and persuade them to give my work some free publicity. At the show last week I devised an inspirational marketing ploy, although my wife thinks I may have got carried away and bitten off more than we can both chew.

Surrounded at the bar by various regional and national newspaper hacks, I proceeded to tell them that they were missing a golden opportunity to unearth a rare treasure. All they ever wrote about, I argued while topping up their glasses with some specially imported homebrew Calvados, were the alleged delights of holidays in overcrowded and overpriced destinations in what I contemptuously

153

dismissed as tourist France. Even when they did produce a feature on Normandy, I said, it is always the posh areas of Calvados such as Honfleur and its overpriced restaurants and sophisticated residents that they bang on about. Why did they not break new ground and come to Real France and see just how much Cotentin has to offer? Warming to my theme and the *calva* samples I was sharing with the press pack, I challenged them all to come on an all-expenses paid voyage of discovery to my home region. I would give them Cotentin on a plate, and they would be doing themselves and their readers a favour by spending a wonderful weekend in a hitherto undiscovered holidaymaker's paradise. Unfortunately, at least half of the reporters present were so enthused by my rhetoric that they agreed to my proposal on the spot. When I woke up in our hotel room the following morning with a hangover, my wife reminded me that all we had to do now was (a) find the money to pay for the event, and (b) think of somewhere to take our guests which would live up to my glowing description of Cotentin as the undiscovered jewel of Normandy.

*   *   *   *   *

It is the day of the press pack's visit, and I am feeling somewhat nervous about the outcome. We are in Cherbourg ferry terminal, awaiting the arrival of the cream of newspaper and magazine travel writers from around Britain. All we need now is some decent weather and a successful conclusion to the day, which is to take the form of a novelty treasure hunt. After spending a few sleepless nights and some long days with a map of our region, I have come up with an idea which, if all goes well, will promote both the attractions of Cotentin as a short-stay holiday destination, and bare-facedly plug our books about our adventures here. Theoretically, our guests will arrive on the overnight boat, take breakfast in the terminal, then race off in their cars with a map of the peninsula and a sheet of paper bearing cryptic clues and directions to places of interest in the area. If they don't get lost, break down or become stuck behind a herd of cows in a lane somewhere along the way, they will arrive at the Café de Paris in Bricquebec in time for a glass or two of Calvados and a meeting with all the local characters featured in my books. My touch of inspiration was to call the event a fox hunt, and arrange for René Ribet to be on hand to sign copies of my book about him. Best of all, the cost of the trip is being met by a somewhat bemused Cotentin tourist board, and P&O Ferries have kindly pitched in to provide the crossing and prizes for the first hacks to pass the winning post.

As we wait at the quayside for the *Pride of Cherbourg* to arrive, it starts to rain, and my wife asks if I have thought about any further and more serious events which could put a dampener on the day. When I challenge her to play devil's advocate, she points out that it is quite possible that René Ribet, the actual quarry of the so-called Fox Hunt, may decide to visit the Widow of Négreville instead of Bricquebec this evening. He has a pocketful of spending money I gave him for expenses, and even if he is at our rendezvous, he may well be incapable of speaking to the journalists if and when they arrive. Then there is the possibility of the press pack wandering into the sights of a real hunt, or even being shot by a farmer if they get my clues wrong and trespass on private land. Worse still, what if they are unfamiliar with driving customs in Cotentin, and think they will be safe if they obey the rules of the road as they apply to the rest of France? There could, she says grimly, even be a fatality.

I think about the possibilities, then point out that her worries are needless. The one thing that everybody knows about the publicity business is that no news is bad news. An accidental death or even murder of a journalist would guarantee acres of newsprint, and could account for thousands of extra copies of our books being sold this year.

*   *   *   *   *

By mid-morning, I find myself laying belly down in the rolling dunes at the seaside resort of Carteret. If all has gone well, the press pack will have collected specially marked mussel shells from the fishing village of Barfleur, scaled the heights at La Pernelle in search of the smallest town hall in Normandy (if not all France) and be well on their way to Carteret to find the next clue, which is in a bottle I have secreted in the seafront toilets directly below our observation point. With my binoculars trained on the toilet block to watch for their arrival, I am heavily disguised in my Father Christmas mask, with dark glasses and a giant beret for good measure. Beside me, the elegant public relations lady from P&O Ferries is dusting sand from her designer coat, and wearing the look of someone who is wondering just what she has let herself in for, and what are the implications for her future if the day gets any more bizarre. Her mood and confidence in the PR value of the event has not been improved by the incident with an angry parent after his small daughter stumbled upon our hiding place and ran screaming from my offer of a sweetie to buy her silence.

*   *   *   *   *

It is the early hours of the next day, and Donella, the ferry lady and I are sitting on a low wall in the square at Bricquebec. A cold rain is falling but we are oblivious to its sting. Against all odds, the press pack hunt has gone better than we dared hope, or the lady from P&O had dared expect after I was cautioned by the local policeman for spying on innocent holiday makers using the toilets at Carteret. Then there had been the unfortunate incident when one of the press pack had been arrested for looking under the doors of the cubicles in the Gents in search of the bottle with the message in it. After we had affected his release, the hunt was on again, and the journalists had virtually all fallen in to the spirit of the chase. Between them, they had also fallen in to at least one river, a pond and a forest of brambles as they scoured the Cotentin countryside for clues before arriving bloody but unbeaten at Bricquebec to beard the Fox in his den. To everyone's surprise

René Ribet was there and on his best behaviour. He was also wearing his best suit and had shaved and combed his hair especially for the occasion, which rather spoiled the characterful rustic effect I had been hoping for. Later, there had been a splendid dinner at the hotel in the castle, a long speech of welcome from a representative of the Cotentin Tourist Board, and a much longer selection of traditional country airs from a man with a guitar and a very untraditional pork pie hat.

After the singer had been persuaded to take his final bow, it was time for the prizes to be awarded, and our guests to put on the strings of onions and silly hats I had persuaded the PR lady they would enjoy wearing. Then it was off on a tour of the nightlife of Bricquebec, which did not take long. Our night ended spectacularly at the bar which is the haunt of the local bikers we have dubbed The Wild Bunch, but who in reality are a group of overly polite youths who spend the evenings looking admiringly at each other's mopeds.

Next morning, we stood at the hotel doors and saw our guests off. Some were still wearing their silly hats and onion strings, and all looked slightly dazed as a result of their wild weekend. Each of them promised to do what they could to tell their readers exactly what Cotentin had to offer the sophisticated traveller, and one took the trouble to tell me what an unforgettable and rewarding trip it had been. Normally, he said, he and his colleagues would be whisked away on a jet to some exotic location where they would be put up in five-star accommodation and force-fed on gourmet delicacies. I was obviously a master in reverse marketing, and it had made a real change to have been our guests. When his sprained wrist got better, he would certainly do his best to do justice to his story about their weekend in pursuit of the Fox of Cotentin. In the meantime, he was looking forward to becoming the owner of the charming little cottage that René Ribet had agreed to sell him. It seemed a real snip at the £10,000 he had beaten our friend down to during some hard late-night bargaining after the rest of us had gone to bed. He hoped that the transaction wouldn't be seen by the local people as a worldly-wise top newspaper man from London taking advantage of a gullible countryman, and that René will be able to find somewhere else to live with not too much trouble.

I tell him not to worry, and hope that he will write the piece publicising our book and the area before he finds out that René's cottage actually belongs to the farmer on whose land it stands.

*   *   *   *   *

I have unwittingly caused quite a stir in the village. Making a post-hunt visit to Ghislaine's bar, I find that all the talk at this morning's Jolly Boys Club meeting was of a rumour that wife-swapping parties have been taking place in St Jacques de Néhou during the long winter months. I try to make a joke and explain that I once went to a wife-swapping orgy in England, but the best offer I received was a washing machine. After solemnly debating my experience, the JBC members pass a motion to place an advertisement in the local paper so they can see what valuable household goods they might get in exchange for their spouses.

*   *   *   *   *

After all the fuss and excitement of the Fox Hunt, we are visiting friends for a relaxing weekend by the seaside.

Ste Mère Eglise is an otherwise unremarkable town on the eastern coast of the peninsula, but was the scene of some of the fiercest fighting during the D-Day landings. Most people may not remember the name of the place, but will know of the bizarre incident when an American paratrooper snagged his parachute on the church steeple and hung there for hours before being rescued. He was deafened by the church bells, but escaped death in spite of hundreds of Germans taking pot shots at him from below. To

158

commemorate the liberation of the town and remind people of the sacrifices made to win freedom, a parachute is draped from the steeple of the church at Ste Mère Eglise on special occasions throughout the year.

As we pull up in the square, I see that the parachute is in place, and try to imagine what it must have been like to be trapped up there with people shooting at you like a china plate at the fun fair.

We walk across the cobbles towards the bar where we are meeting our friends and the studs on the soles of my boots echo in the evening air. The church bells begin to ring the Angelus, and I hear music coming through the open window of a car parked outside the café. It is the jaunty film theme from *The Longest Day*, and I feel the hairs on the back of my neck bristle. Somewhere in my head I hear the sound of bullets and people screaming as madness and death visited this peaceful square. I had forgotten that today is June 6th.

*   *   *   *   *

More reminders of Cotentin at war as we spend an evening with Jack and Mary Harry. In a past life, the couple ran a thriving retail business in Norfolk. Now, the pace of their lives is gentler and very different. Their home is the last house along a track which literally ends in the *marais du Cotentin*, a huge and desolate marshland which almost bisects the peninsula. Once, *Le Phare* was a stopping-off point for barges on their way to and from Paris. Now, lucky B&B visitors to the Harry's home can sit on the balcony with a glass in hand, watching the Douve meander endlessly by as they dream their own dreams of escaping to a new life in France.

This evening, the talk turns to local memories of the Occupation, and Jack explains that the *marais* was a major dropping zone for Allied parachutists during the D-Day invasion. Many drowned in the treacherous marshlands. Some were impaled on the thousands of metal stakes known with the grimmest of black humour as Rommel's asparagus. Jack also shows me where a simple but poignant monument marks the grave of a Spitfire which came down during the fighting. Before the Germans could reach the site of the crash, a fisherman had reclaimed the body of the young pilot and given it a secret and dignified burial. The local people also took part of the wreckage to make a tribute to their fallen ally. Each year pupils from the pilot's school visit the monument to maintain it, and to keep alive the memory of a young man who gave his all for another land.

As the setting sun catches the wings of the replica atop the Spitfire monument, we think of how distant and yet recent are the times when ordinary people from other lands fought and died for the freedom of this beautiful country and its people.

To lighten our mood, Jack tells me a joke he heard from his neighbour that day as they talked about the war years in Normandy. It is very French, and concerns Hitler's alleged masterplan to invade England. Summoning General Rommel, the Führer explained his ingenious idea. The whole German army, he said, would be drawn up in a single line on the beaches of Calais. They would then be ordered to wade into the sea, fill their field-issue mugs, and begin to drink. Eventually, the Channel would run dry, and the army could march on Dover without even getting its feet wet. In spite of Rommel's reservations, he saw that his leader's orders were carried out to the letter, and watched as the army began its impossible task. After three days had passed and only the tide had lowered the waters, Rommel was faced with the problem of either telling the Führer he was mad, or admitting failure. His solution was to visit Hitler and report that he had been watching the Dover coastline through binoculars, and had discovered a problem. On the distant shore he had seen the entire British army lined up, and they too were knee-deep in the waters of the Channel. Behind them on the beach was Field-Marshall

Montgomery, executing his unspeakable counter-attack. The actions by the man and his army were typically underhand and unsporting, said the Desert Fox. Each time the order was given for the German troops to dip their mugs into the sea and lift them to their lips, the order would go out to the British soldiers to unzip their flies and restore the level of the Channel. This, of course, was the only reason that the Führer's brilliant strategy was doomed to failure.

We go in to dinner, and as I admire the Harry's work on the restoration of *Le Phare*, Mary confesses that she may have made her own small contribution to inter-cultural confusion. As she showed a local carpenter round the house last week, he had admired the wooden dado rails running at waist-height along the passage wall, and she had told him what she thought they were known as in England. After checking with her husband, Mary realised she had made a slip of the tongue. Now, she is haunted by mental images of the carpenter asking his customers if they would like an English-style dildo anywhere on the premises.

Visiting Times

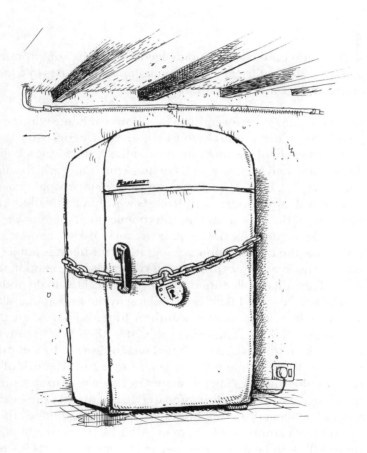

It is a truth universally acknowledged by French property owners that their circle of friends and acquaintances increases by a factor of ten as the summer months approach.

Given the going rate for hiring a farmhouse in France during the peak period, there is no better incentive for people to dig out their address books as thoughts turn to the year's foreign holiday destination, and then to who has a house in France which can be taken over for free. At La Puce, our phone starts ringing as the first snowdrops appear, and friends who haven't called once throughout the long winter months queue up to ask how we are, and chide us gently for not keeping in touch. We will know exactly which way the conversation is going to turn when the subject of summer holidays comes up, and our callers casually mention their plans. They will usually announce they have decided to do nothing special this year, and have been talking in the pub about taking a cottage in France for the month of June, July or August. Or sometimes all three. They will be joined by their best friends and family, which will make a combined total of five adults and twelve children. Rather than go somewhere nice in the south of the country, they have decided to slum it in Normandy to save on the travelling, and are therefore prepared to put up with the weather and lack of scenery and sophistication. Considering these criteria, our friends naturally thought of us. After this flattering build-up, there will then be an obvious pause as our caller waits for us to get the plot and come up with the invitation. When it is not forthcoming, it will be the full-frontal attack.

'Actually,' he or she will say, 'we were wondering about staying with you - if that's alright? It would be fun, and we'd be prepared to chip in with the food and drink and other costs, of course.'

This, as any seasoned French property owner knows, is actually code for:

'Look, you live there for free anyway, and we will be doing you a favour by brightening up your miserable lives with our company. As to sharing the costs, we will arrive with a bottle of cheap wine and a box of chocolates, then eat you out of house and home and criticise your furniture, cooking, wallpaper and toilet facilities after we have left. Apart from chopping down at least two trees and performing operations on your dog, our children will spend every day on the phone to their friends in far-flung corners of the world, telling them what a lousy time they are having with the wrinklies. We will expect you to keep us entertained day and night, and when it's all over we will spend the next year finding fault with our time at your scruffy home and boring surroundings, and wishing we had gone to Disneyland for a proper holiday.'

In the early years and before we learned the ropes and the true cost of having friends to stay, we found it difficult to think up a reasonable excuse for turning freeloaders down. As a result, they came in droves. It even got to a point of us moving out for a month to make more room, and inviting our guests to treat our home like their own. Unfortunately, all too many of them did just that.

Nowadays we have learned our lessons, and have a list of acid retorts by the phone for when the calls begin to come. According to the circumstances and what we think of the caller, our response will be:

a) What a shame you didn't call earlier - we've just invited some real friends to stay for the entire summer.

165

b) Sorry, but this year we're fully booked with paying guests instead of freeloaders like you.

c) We've sold La Puce and will be long gone by the time you want to come, but we hear the new owners are charging very reasonable rates for B&B in the caravan.

d) Unfortunately, the farmhouse has been burned down by Basque terrorists with the wrong map.

e) The Black Death has just swept through the village, and the whole of the area is under quarantine for the next six months, with trespassers to be shot on sight.

This may seem a little extreme, but you have to understand how tenacious freeloaders can be. Besides, given the circumstances, accommodation in our part of Normandy is shortly going to be at an all-time premium.

For the first time ever, England is to be included as a stage in the *Tour de France*, and for the first - and probably last - time ever, the route passes through the Cotentin. Even more exciting, the race procession will be going straight past the front door of our farmhouse. Centuries ago, pilgrims followed the scallop shell signpost past La Puce on their way from Cherbourg to join the *Santiago de Compostela* trail to Spain. In my lifetime, tanks trundled along the mill track, Spitfires and Hurricanes screamed overhead, and men fought and died on the road beyond our gate. Soon, the cycling gods of France and lesser beings from the rest of Europe will hurtle fleetingly by our front door, their bottoms in the air and their eyes on the shining road ahead. When the race goes by, La Puce will once again be a silent witness to another stage in the long and eventful history of the Cotentin.

Ever since the route past the crossroads leading off the main road to Néhou and St Jacques de Néhou was confirmed, the commune has been in a fever of excitement. To even begin to understand the significance and impact of the news, a Briton with no particular interest in cycle racing would first have to grasp the status of the sport in France, the importance of the event itself, and what it will mean for our community to be a part of it.

Apart from the prestige for the regions included in the route, the thought of having his area and perhaps even his village appearing on television around the world is almost too much for the average Frenchman to bear. To learn that the *Tour de France* is actually going past your house could be likened to an English soccer fanatic getting a phone call from the FA asking if it would be alright for this year's Cup Final to be played in his back garden.

Already, policy committees, strategy think-tanks and action groups have been set up to ensure that Néhou gets its fair share of the reflected glory, and spies have been sent out to discover how our rival village of St Jacques de Néhou is planning to steal our thunder. For once, the result of our stage and even the race itself has become insignficant. The real yellow jersey and winner's laurel will go to which of the two villages puts on the best show.

The world will be watching, and Néhou must be ready.

For months now, the residents of both villages have been working around the clock to outdo each other in giving their homes and gardens a complete makeover. Even though neither community is within a mile of the route, goats, chickens and pigs and their living accommodation have been banished to back yards, new curtain material has been purchased by the kilometre, and there is even a local ordinance to be rushed through banning cows from the roads for the week of the race.

Along the actual route from Bricquebec to St-Sauveur, there is even more frantic activity. House fronts are being whitewashed, gardens filled to overflowing with instant and exotic blooms where

167

once a pile of logs and an abandoned car were the only decoration. Flagpoles have been erected every hundred metres along the road, the hedges regimentally trimmed, dead animals removed from ditches, and verges manicured to within an inch of their lives. I have even had a deputation from the special Race Highways committee asking me if I will attend to the broken hinge on our yard gate, and there is talk of either totally rebuilding Mr Moineau's dilapidated cottage, or simply blowing it up so it will not give a bad impression of our area.

It also seems that our village of Néhou has for some reason called upon the special skills of René Ribet to help with the preparations. Last week, I saw the mayoral tractor outside the Fox's tumbledown cottage, and he has been in great demand at every official committee meeting. Just yesterday, I was rather hurt to arrive at the Bar Ghislaine and find an unscheduled meeting of the Jolly Boys Club in full flood. Inexplicably, Ghislaine was handing René what appeared to be a free drink, and she was actually smiling archly at him. The conversation stopped dead as I walked in, then my fellow members made some lame excuse about having to convene a special Tour meeting. Being English, they naturally thought I would not be interested in the Greatest Race On Earth. As I left in a huff, I heard someone mutter something about it being a special 'steering' committee, and a gale of laughter followed me out of the door. Something is obviously afoot, and René Ribet is undoubtedly behind it. Although it appears not to involve La Puce or my money, I am feeling understandably nervous, and my trepidation increases as the big day approaches. René, meanwhile, is obviously revelling in the situation and his new-found popularity.

The attention he is getting seems to have gone straight to his head, and he has taken to entering the local bars wearing dark glasses and with his donkey jacket draped across his shoulders like a famous impresario or film producer. I am even worried that, as the time for the Race approaches, no tents, caravans or scaffolding for TV cameras have sprouted in my roadside fields. My first thought on hearing about the route was that René would already be busily auctioning off prime viewing areas at La Puce to the highest bidder. Some of the houses further along the road have been rented out for incredible sums for the week leading up to the raceday, and it is rumoured that our local carpenter is building a spectator gallery in his yard, with seats to be sold to the highest bidder. I think he will have to give out binoculars with the places, as his premises are at least a mile away from the road where the action will be taking place. There is also gossip that a farmer down the road from us is busily converting his milking parlour into a hospitality centre for corporate entertainment, and it is somehow disturbing that René has not come to me with a single suggestion as to how we can both make a fortune out of the event. When we met last week, I tried to draw him into the open by saying that I may be offering the farmhouse to my press pack friends from the Fox Hunt, but he only smiled slyly and advised me not to bother. Something is going on, and all the signs are that my wily friend has got his nose firmly on the scent of a kill.

Tour de Force

NB: This final section is the result of a dream after a particularly heavy night at the Bar Ghislaine, followed by a particularly heavy supper of goat's cheese Welsh Rarebit. The Tour de France did in fact pass our door, but the sequence of events described here did not happen in real life.

The big day has arrived, and we are ready to play host to the greatest cycle race in the world.

Within the hour, the travelling circus that is the Tour de France will speed along the D900 and past the roadside farmhouse at La Puce. For once it is literally true to say that excitement is at fever pitch, as every single worker in the area seems to have gone down with a mysterious virus and all the shops and businesses have closed for the day. Even I am caught up in the mood of joyous anticipation as we wait for the fun to start. The riders themselves will flash by La Puce in moments, but the cavalcade of entertainment will last for nearly an hour. First will come the advance party, with police motorcyclists specially chosen for their menacing looks ensuring the way ahead is clear. They will be followed by the promotional parade, with a fleet of sponsored vehicles all sounding their horns and playing unintelligible advertisements and different but equally awful French pop tunes. Leaning from the cars and vans will be pretty girls in branded T-shirts, waving, smiling and throwing free samples to the eager crowd. I can see the attraction of the soft drink and chocolate bar gifts, but wait with interest to see exactly what the company promoting sanitary towels will be tossing at the spectators. After the carnival will come the official vehicles, crammed with everyone who has found an excuse to get in on the act. More unintelligible announcements will be blaring from loudspeakers almost as big as the cars that carry them, and a giant travelling clock will be keeping us all up to speed with how the riders are doing. And everywhere, there will be pompous little men in dark glasses and fluorescent safety bibs. They will be proudly displaying their official badges and clipboards, and doing all they can to get in the way and spoil our fun. At last and when they have cautioned enough spectators for having their toes in the road or eating oranges in a dangerous manner they will move on, and the way will be clear for our knights of the road.

But all this will come later. For now, the verges alongside the road past La Puce are filled with more people than I thought lived in the whole of the region. Or at least, the St Jacques de Néhou side of the road is filled with people. By tradition and for reasons of personal safety, the occupants of the rival villages stay religiously to their side of the crossroads, and even today they will obviously not be breaking with custom. St Jacques de Néhou lies a mile to the west of the main road, and Néhou the same distance to the east, and both lead a completely separate existence. Each village has its own church, school, shop and mayor, and each commune regards the other with a deep and abiding distrust, nurtured carefully over the centuries. Nobody knows exactly what momentous event caused the two similarly-named villages to be in such a permanent state of antipathy, and nobody seems to care. Old Pierrot says that it is all to do with our rival village of St Jacques being named after a proper French saint, while we drew the short straw with a second division player. Even worse, our man is the patron saint of a foreign country. I discovered shortly after arriving at La Puce that the full and official name of our village is actually St Georges de Néhou, and am still disappointed that my namesake is never mentioned or acknowledged; even the maps and official signposts to Néhou do not bear the prefix. Perhaps the relative status of the two saints is the cause of the enmity between our two communities, or perhaps it is just that everyone secretly enjoys the permanent state of hostility. Last year, it was even proposed that a frontier barrier should be placed at our side of the crossroads, but our committee couldn't find any volunteers to man it twenty-four hours a day, so the scheme was dropped.

Today, though, there seems to be no need for any barriers to keep the two factions apart. While their side of the road is occupied by every member of the St Jacques community who can stand, and even some who cannot, I do not recognise a single villager from Néhou amongst the throng opposite. Perhaps they have taken up their positions nearer to the crossroads, or perhaps they are leaving it to the last minute to make a grand entrance and upstage the rival commune. If so, they are leaving it rather late. Word has spread through the crowd that the race has already sped through Bricquebec, and that the outriders will be with us in minutes. Even more puzzling to me than the absence of the Néhou community, however, is the complete lack of television cameras or press photographers along our part of the route. The upper fields of La Puce start at the bend immediately after the crossroads to St Jacques and Néhou, and skirt a particularly wide and straight section of the highway for more than half a mile. The road also runs downhill, and I would have thought our raised fields would have offered a perfect vantage point. But there is no sign of a single satellite van, camera crew or even photographer, so they must have found a better spot further back down the route. Apart from the natural disappointment of pictures of La Puce not being flashed around the world, my erection of a huge roadside sign advertising Victor the Volvo for sale and giving our international telephone number has obviously been a complete waste of time.

But now the great moment draws near, and I help Donella up the stepladder resting precariously on our courtyard wall. If I cannot hire this prime location and the ladder out for a hundred times its worth to a member of the visual media, we might as well take advantage of it ourselves.

As we make ourselves comfortable, a momentary hush falls along our section of the route, followed by a buzz of excitement. In the distance, we hear the steady drone of motorcycles, and the tinny distorted babble of at least six sponsors trying to get their messages across. Along the route, the crowd surges forward, and the more daring even slip beneath the barriers and run into the road to be the first to declare a sighting. Strangely, the distant sound of the approaching procession begins to grow fainter rather than louder, and silence returns to our stretch of the route. A thousand lips are pouted and eyebrows raised, and the crowd performs a particularly gallic version of the Mexican Wave as mass shoulder-shrugging breaks out. On the far side of the road, the mayor of St Jacques decides it is time to assert his authority and investigate the mystery. Breaking with a hundred years of tradition, he strides across the road, nods at my wife, and asks stiffly if he can borrow our stepladder for official business. For a moment, I think about asking him to sign a hire agreement, but realise that the situation demands compromise and co-operation, and hand it over the wall. The mayor returns to the middle of the highway, sets up the stepladder and climbs to the top. After peering in the direction from which the race should be approaching, he frowns, then raises both arms to signal silence. We obey, and all is still.

From the distance, we hear a strange sound. It is a laboured and rhythmic squeaking. The crowd becomes even quieter, and the mysterious noise grows steadily louder. Suddenly, a little child by our gatepost can bear the suspense no longer, and breaking away from his mother's side he darts out in to the road and runs back towards the bend leading to the crossroads. After a moment, his distant figure goes into a wild jig of excitement, and he rushes back to tell us the good news. The race is here, and the champion is coming!

There is another surge as the crowd push forward against the barriers, and a lone figure rounds the bend. But it is not a lithe young man in lycra sportswear, pedalling for all his worth towards the yellow jersey and his eternal claim to fame. It is Mike the Bike, on his way to St Sauveur and his weekly benefit cheque. Michel is the first member of the Néhou community I have seen today, and he is obviously not going to change his routine, race or no race.

As we watch in stunned silence, Michel pedals laboriously along the centre of the highway, deep in his own thoughts as he pushes his old bicycle to the limits to reach the post office before lunchtime closing.

Nearing our gate, he looks up as if aware of his audience for the first time. Gruffly, he bids me good day, and then concentrates again on forcing the rusty pedals round. As he navigates around the stepladder in the middle of the road and exchanges glares with the mayor of St Jacques, I call out and ask him if he has seen any sign of the Tour. He looks at me as if I am mad and asks why we are wasting our time with the nincompoops from St Jacques. The Race has already passed, he wheezes, and has made him late for a vital appointment. It took at least ten minutes for him to reach the crossroads, and all those bloody fools with their arses in the air were going the wrong way. By now, unless they have realised their mistake, they will have passed through Néhou and be halfway to Calvados.

* * * * *

There is uproar in the road outside, and we have retreated to the safety of the cellar of the farmhouse. The greatest cycle race in the world has been sabotaged, and the villagers of St Jacques already think they know who is to blame.

Moments after Mike the Bike told us that the Tour de France had gone the wrong way, the obviously distraught part-time policeman at St Jacques arrived on his official moped to report to the mayor. All had been going smoothly, he had said, until the convoy leaders had reached the crossroads leading to the two villages. There, the police outriders found a tractor and badly-damaged car completely blocking the route. The local fire brigade and paramedic team were already at the scene, and were tending the injured with great zeal. The advance party of security guards had returned back along the route to warn the race marshall, and in their absence, other race officials had suddenly appeared and gone into action. A barrier and deviation sign had been hastily erected, and the police outriders had been despatched to clear the route of the diversion back on to the main road. Moments later, the lead cars had arrived, been frantically waved on to the new route, and the riders had naturally followed the procession. At first, it had appeared that the legendary French attributes of decisiveness and keeping a cool head in a crisis had come into their own and averted a disaster. It was not until the race had passed and was safely back on the main road to St Sauveur that questions began to be asked by those left behind. Who, for example, had taken the decision to re-route the race through Néhou rather than St Jacques, a course which would have brought the riders back to the highway much sooner? Why had the streets of Néhou been lined with flag-waving and cheering villagers who could not have known that the deviation was going to take place? Along the same line of reasoning, what about the large and painstakingly prepared banner welcoming the race and the world to Néhou? Even more suspiciously, why were all the camera crews and press photographers for that stage of the race set up and ready for action in Néhou rather than on the planned route? A local inquiry was already under way, and blame would doubtless be apportioned in due course. Tragically, the policeman said, he had been responding to a hoax call regarding a pig trapped up a tree at St Jacques at the crucial time. Otherwise, he would obviously have spotted the inconsistencies as the drama was unfolding.

Now, questions would obviously have to be asked at the highest level, and an investigation would need to be launched by the nation's internal security forces. Already, there was talk of an international conspiracy to humiliate France in the eyes of the world, or even give an unfair advantage to a foreign competitor. According to the news reports, the incident would not mar or affect the result of the Cotentin stage, as the illicit diversion had been exactly the same distance as the proper route along the D900. But the real damage had been done locally. The villagers of St Jacques had been deprived of their chance to see the race go by, and worst of all, Néhou had been the focus of attention of the whole world as the riders whizzed through its mean streets. The old enemy would be crowing about their moment of fame for years, and it was reported that directors of several rival TV companies had been seen negotiating for the rights to make a drama-documentary about the incident. The Néhou representative had been wearing dark glasses and a ridiculous Father Christmas false beard, but the way he had forced the offers up and run rings around the high-powered executives made it perfectly clear who was behind the disguise and the conspiracy. Whatever the outcome of the enquiry, the people of St Jacques were wise to the ways of the countryside, and knew how to recognise the tell-tale signs that a fox had been at work...

*   *   *   *   *

It is later on the same day, and the situation has calmed. I have been able to escape undetected from the farmhouse at La Puce, and have arrived at the Bar Ghislaine to find the mother of all parties in full swing.

In one corner, a villager who is also a senior member of the St Sauveur fire brigade and paramedic squad is sharing a table and a drink with Madame Ghislaine's husband. Bernard has a gory bandage around his temples, but the stain looks more like red wine than blood. Nearby, several members of the Jolly Boys Club are standing in a huddle with Dodgy Didier, and all look very pleased with themselves. Marcel Bernard is wearing a fluorescent Race Official bib, and I note from the date on the back that it is from last year's event. A crowd of TV types are gathered at the bar, and René Ribet is showing them how to play a local game of chance involving a pair of home-made dice. As I have learned to my cost in the past, the main rule of the game is that the rules change dependent on the outcome of each cast, and René is the only one who knows the exact details.

Through the open door to the back room, I can see Madame Ghislaine and the mayor of Néhou sitting at a table. They are counting a huge pile of money, and it is the second time this week that I have seen Ghislaine smile. As I order a drink, Old Pierrot tells me that the fund for the village school has soared dramatically as a result of the day's activities. The press photographers and TV crews paid handsomely for their allotted places, and the auction for the use of Madame Ghislaine's bedroom as the best filming point raised more than the value of the whole building. Now, the committee will not only be able to buy a complete set of new school desks and books, but will have more than enough to build a new wing to put them in. Officially, the extension will be known as the *Salle de Tour*, but it has already been dubbed by the Jolly Boys Club as The Hall of The Fox.

*   *   *   *   *

It is approaching midnight, but the celebrations show no sign of abating. Corks pop as the mayor delivers a speech of tribute to the architect of the day's triumph and makes an obviously in-joke about the effectiveness of our Steering Committee. Ice-cold cider froths and sparkles as the Normandy champagne flows, and we prepare to salute the hero of the day. I pick up a traditional stone cider-mug and look across the crowded bar to where René stands on a chair by the fireplace. He has finally removed his dark glasses, and as our eyes meet, my friend nods, smiles and sends me a huge pantomime wink.

This time next week we both know he will be in trouble with any or all of the villagers, but tonight the Fox of Cotentin is truly the toast of Néhou.

Epilogue

Autumn has arrived, and another eventful year at La Puce is drawing to a close. Soon, our non-paying guests will be settling down for the long winter ahead, or packing their bags and heading south. My wife will be sad to see them leave, but she knows that they will do their best to return with the Spring.

Elsewhere, all our friends will be making plans for the long, hard months ahead and reflecting on the dying year and how it has treated them.

Today, we had news that Madge The Hornet Woman has come to a satisfactory settlement with the local fire brigade. They have promised to leave her in peace, and she has not told them that she has persuaded another colony to set up home in her attic. In her letter, she apologised for the shaky handwriting, and says it is her age. I think she has probably been smoking too many of her home-grown cigarettes. We have also had a call from Les Miserable's wife Ono, who says that things are going quite well, apart from last month's fire, and Moondance and Zak have faxed to say they now have a whole dormitory of slippers in their bedroom. In Bricquebec, our lonely missionary friend is still trying to preach to the otherwise converted, and in the Café de Paris, Freddo and his regulars are still planning their haggis-shooting trip to Scotland.

On the coast, Mike and Rita have had a successful season, and report that there have been no further unfortunate mistakes with the pedal-bin in the men's toilet.

At the Bar Ghislaine, the Jolly Boys Club is flourishing, and we have not lost a member this year. Old Pierrot went missing for a couple of weeks in the late summer, but reappeared to say he had merely been fishing for ormers with the Widow of Négreville, and been caught when the tide came in.

And René is still being René. As suspected, it did not take him long to blot his copybook in Néhou, and he has been laying low until Madame Ghislaine forgives him.

As for us and our lives together, I have been trying to persuade my wife that it is time to move on. I love La Puce and everything about our tiny corner of the Cotentin almost as much as she does, but life is short and we are no longer young. Perhaps it is watching the birds fly off to new and different places, or perhaps I just want to see what is round the next bend. Perhaps it is that we are so happy here that I am too afraid to stay. For whatever reason, the mood is upon me, and I have asked Donella to at least think about the new adventures which could lay ahead if we take the moment.

Whatever happens to us and wherever we may go in the coming months and years, one thing is certain. We will always remember our time at the Mill of the Flea with a deep affection and gratitude for what we have learned about life in this small and very special rural community.

And, of course, what we have learned about ourselves in the process.

THE END

Home & Dry in France
follows the early adventures
of George and Donella East
as the innocents abroad
search for a home in
France, discover the Little
Jewel, and finally arrive at
the Mill of the Flea.

If you've ever toyed with
the idea of owning some
small corner of a foreign
field, you'll find this best-
selling book required
reading. If you're an
armchair traveller in search
of no more than a rattling
good read, you'll find *Home
& Dry in France* the perfect
travelling companion…

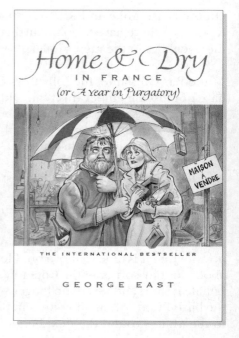

*"Find all those 'How to buy a house in France' books dull and dreary?
Have a go at this one. It's so different you'll be entranced from page one
until the end. I literally laughed until I cried."*

France in Print

Home & Dry in France by George East   **ISBN: 0 9523635 0 X**

RRP: £6.99

*La Puce Publications (UK): 87 Laburnum Grove, Portsmouth PO2 0HG
Telephone: (023) 92 678148*

René & Me is the second book in the *French Letters* trilogy, and charts a memorable year as the author and his wife attempt to survive on their wits at the Mill of the Flea.

As our unlikely heroes battle to succeed with doomed schemes for trout farming with no trout and metal-detecting weekends to discover the miller's secret hoard, René Ribet moves on to their land and in to their lives.

During a year of adventures as improbable as they are true, the Easts discover why their friend is known as The Fox of Cotentin, and where the real treasure of La Puce is to be found...

"When such experiences are presented by a raconteur of George East's stature, few people could fail to ignore all else until the book is devoured to the very last page..."

Living France Magazine

René & Me by George East   **ISBN: 0 9523635 1 8**

RRP: £6.99

La Puce Publications (UK): 87 Laburnum Grove, Portsmouth PO2 0HG
Telephone: (023) 92 678148